John B. Keane is one of Ireland's best-loved humorous writers and is recognised as a major Irish playwright. He has written many bestsellers including *The Contractors, Durango, A High Meadow, The Celebrated Letters of John B. Keane, The Field, Sive, Big Maggie* and *The Year of the Hiker*. Films have been made of *The Field* and *Durango*.

John B. Keane

Moll

The Chastitute

Many Young Men of Twenty
A Bar-Room Sketch

MERCIER PRESS

Mercier Press
PO Box 5, 5 French Church Street, Cork
16 Hume Street, Dublin 1

Trade enquiries to CMD DISTRIBUTION,
55a Spruce Avenue, Stillorgan Industrial Park, Blackrock, Dublin

© John B. Keane

ISBN 1 85635 264 1
A CIP record for this book is available from the British Library.

10 9 8 7 6 5 4 3 2 1

The Arts Council
An Chomhairle Ealaíon

The Publishers gratefully acknowledge the financial assistance of
The Arts Council/An Chomhairle Ealaíon

Printed in Ireland by Colour Books Ltd.

CONTENTS

MOLL

This revised version of *Moll* was first presented by Groundwork in association with Gaiety Entertainments at the Gaiety Theatre on 10 June 1991.

Father Brest	Barry McGovern
Bridgie Andover	Joan Brosnan Walsh
Canon Pratt	Mick Lally
Father Loran	Ronan Smith
Moll	Pat Leavy
Ulick	Micheál Ó Briain
The Bishop	Derry Power

Director	Brian de Salvo
Designer	Bláithín Sheerin
Lighting	Rupert Murray
Producers	Ben Barnes
	Arthur Lappin
Executive producer	Ronan Smith

New revised text edited by Ben Barnes

Act One

Scene One

To set a scene or provide an amusing philosophical commentary on the preceding one, a series of extracts from Canon Pratt's diary have been selected with appropriate accompanying action on the fore-stage. These 'front cloth' vignettes also enable the stage to be set for the following scene and ensure a continual flow of action.

Pratt After the new money came things were never the same at the presbytery. Till then summers came and summers went each one much like the last. Ballast was a poor parish but God was good and even the weather was good sometimes and we went about our duties without a bother on us.

Until the summer of that fateful year of our Lord 1971 when the money went decimal. Oh it had a most shocking and deleterious effect on some people. Why else would our housekeeper of twenty years, the honest, sober, industrious and respectable Letitia Bottomley suddenly up and marry an American tourist and emigrate to New Jersey in the United States of America, there to open a diner which she entitled 'The Black Bottom Bistro'?

Yirra, 'twas the decimal money that drove the poor woman demented and left us with the onerous duty of finding a new housekeeper …

The curtain rises to reveal the dining cum sitting-room of the parochial house in the town and parish of Ballast. Seated at one end of a large table to left of audience but facing them for the most part are three priests. Two are young whereas the one in the middle is elderly and exhibits the purple of a canon here and there. Seated at the other end of the table at right of audience but fully facing them is a large, dour woman of advanced years. She is Miss Andover. She wears hat and coat and has a large handbag held tightly in front of her. The curates are Fr Loran, the younger and Fr Brest, the older. The

9

parish priest is Canon Pratt. In front of the priests are neat files to which they resort from time to time. As the curtain rises the priests and canon are seen to be exchanging whispers and confidences. Miss Andover strains forward trying to catch what they are saying. Fr Brest becomes aware of this and alerts the others who immediately pay full attention to Miss Andover.

Time: One morning not too long ago.

Fr Brest It says here, Miss Andover, in this most recent reference from the late Fr Hennessy that you take a drink on occasion. Does this mean intoxicating drink?

Miss Andover *(Looks away when she answers)* For all I take of it father, I don't know why he mentioned it at all, the Lord be good to the man.

Fr Brest Yes, yes … You do take intoxicating drink however?

Miss Andover On very rare occasions father, barring I had a cold or pains or the like.

Fr Brest I see. *(To others)* Any further questions?

Canon Pratt Supposing you were to get the job Miss Andover, would you require extra help?

Miss Andover Well, I would have to have a maid naturally. There's three of you ….

Canon Pratt And what sort of salary would you be expecting?

Miss Andover God knows canon seeing the way everything's gone up since the money went decimal if I get's the job, I'd need ten pounds a week.

Fr Brest It says here, Miss Andover, that you are a good, natural cook.

Miss Andover I'm all that father.

Fr Brest I'm sure you are. Tell me. What is meant by *natural?*

Miss Andover Yirra, the Lord be good to the poor man father, he always ate what I put in front of him and there was never a word out of him.

Fr Brest I'm sure he did. It's just that the expression is so unusual. *(To others)* These are not the kind of words that automatically link each other. Usually we hear of plain cooks and excellent cooks. I've even heard of simple cooks but a natural cook … now that's a new one.

Fr Loran	*(Entering into the spirit of things)* I see what you mean. Could it be that cooking comes natural to her, that she is a sort of genius at it? *(Uses hand to explain)* Jack Dempsey was a natural fighter and … take Caruso … he was a natural singer, sure Jack Doyle was both. Say a fellow goes out and plays golf for the first time and doesn't miss the ball the first swing … well he's natural. *(There is a sobering cough from Canon Pratt, curates are attentive at once)* Sorry canon.
Fr Brest	*(To Miss Andover)* Now Miss Andover I would like to submit you to a small test.
	(Miss Andover jumps up, almost falls, recovers and sits)
Miss Andover	You won't put a hand on me. I was never touched by the hand of a man …
Fr Brest	It's not a physical test. I'll merely mention a particular word or group of words and you say whatever comes into your mind. Do you understand?
Miss Andover	All right. I'll chance it.
Fr Brest	Wardrobe!
Miss Andover	Bottle of gin!
Fr Brest	Sweet tooth!
Miss Andover	Porter cake!
Fr Brest	Sunday morning!
Miss Andover	Gin and tonic!
Fr Brest	Cold in the nose!
Miss Andover	Bloody Mary!
Canon Pratt	Sacristy!
Miss Andover	Altar wine!
	(All three exchange knowing looks)
Fr Brest	Thank you Miss Andover. We know all we need to know. You'll be hearing from us. *(Exit Miss Andover. Canon Pratt produces a pipe which he proceeds to light. Fr Brest rises and lights a cigarette. Fr Loran reads through a file)* There's a right wan!
Canon Pratt	The standard's dropped. Good housekeepers are not to be had.
Fr Brest	You must remember there's plenty of work in factories and hotels.
Canon Pratt	They don't seem anxious to make a career out of it any

	more. When I was a young man it was a great temptation to widows and spoiled nuns and the likes … but now they prefer the outside.
Fr Brest	But they can have the outside morning, noon and night. A parish priest's housekeeper isn't the same as a nun.
Canon Pratt	*(Thoughtfully)* They used to be. They used to be very like them in manner and in obedience. *(To Brest)* By the way you were on the ball about the drinking.
Fr Brest	I knew her late employer, Fr Dick Hennessy. Dineaway Dick the teachers of the parish used to call him.
Canon Pratt	Why Dineaway?
Fr Brest	Don't you see? He never dined at home.
Canon Pratt	Why didn't he say as much in the reference?
Fr Brest	He couldn't.
Canon Pratt	Why couldn't he?
Fr Brest	Because he wasn't able. The Lord have mercy on the poor man he could never bring himself to say a hard word about anyone.
Canon Pratt	That's why you questioned her about the drink?
Fr Brest	Of course. You may be sure if Dick Hennessy said she took a drink on occasion what he really meant was that she was a cross between a wine-taster and a dipsomaniac.
Canon Pratt	And this business about her being a natural cook?
Fr Brest	That she served up the food natural, that is to say she did not bother much with the cooking of it beforehand.
Canon Pratt	Ah …
Fr Brest	Gentlemen, we're in a spot. Here we were without a trouble in the world, as united as three leaves on a shamrock, and as well disposed to each other as if we were brothers and now we are left to look out for ourselves. You'll never know the true worth of a real housekeeper till she's gone. Losing Miss Bottomley was like losing a mother.
Canon Pratt	*(Reverentially)* Lads, do you remember her pickled tongue? Her beef stew?
Fr Loran	Her shepherd's pie, canon!
Fr Brest	Her stuffed pork!
Fr Loran	Her colcannon, canon!

Canon Pratt	Jasus what she couldn't do with a duck! And lads do you remember her cockle and mussel soup? The smell of it, the taste of it. *(They fall silent, basking in the memory of such culinary delights)* This is torture lads, sheer torture. Where were we?
Fr Loran	*(Holding up a file)* This is the last one.
Canon Pratt	Who is she? Refresh me Joe, will you, like a good man.
Fr Loran	Miss Mollie Kettle age forty-seven.
Fr Brest	Forty-seven, my arse.
Canon Pratt	Well we'll soon find out when we see her. *(To Loran)* Go on father.
Fr Loran	Aged forty-seven. Worked as housekeeper in a boys' school in Liverpool, in an old folks' home in Dublin. Worked for nine years as a housekeeper to Monsignor Patrick MacMerrigan. Now retired. She's been idle for three months.
Canon Pratt	Read MacMerrigan's reference. Biggest windbag in the diocese.
Fr Loran	*(Locates and reads)* 'Miss Maureen (Mollie) Kettle', the Mollie is in brackets, 'came to work for me on the death of my housekeeper Mrs Sarah O'Hara nine years ago on the precise morning of the two thousandth and twentieth anniversary of the battle of Pharsalia. *Quanti est sapere.* She struck me at once as being a woman of integrity. She answered all of my questions satisfactorily and having assured myself that her references were in order and that she had a reasonable knowledge of the True Faith I employed her forthwith. I found her to be a thrifty and exact housekeeper, a good time-keeper and a faithful servant. I found her to be a good cook and a better punch-maker. I know no more of the good woman nor do I need to. *Omne ignotum pro magnifico.'* *(Fr Loran puts letter aside)* That's the lot.
Fr Brest	You were right canon. He is a windbag.
Canon Pratt	To use a golfing metaphor you will understand Phil, if she could endure Monsignor MacMerrigan for nine holes, she will go the full eighteen with me.
Fr Brest	This must be approached coldly. *(Moves to centre of table)* If we lose detachment all we gain is a poor house-

13

	keeper.
Canon Pratt	Of course. Of course. Call her in Joe, like a good man, will you? *(Fr Loran rises and goes to door from where he calls)*
Fr Loran	Miss Kettle, will you please come in? *(He returns to his former position as do others. Enter Moll Kettle. Middle-aged. Wears hat and coat, carries handbag)*
Fr Brest	*(Indicates chair vacated by Miss Andover)* Please be seated. *(Moll takes a seat and waits, smiling serenely in all directions. Coughs)* Well now. It's a nice day out Miss Kettle, isn't it?
Moll	It is, thanks be to God, a very nice day entirely canon.
Canon Pratt	Allow me to introduce my two curates, Fr Brest and Fr Loran. It's possible they may want to ask a question or two but be at your ease, be at your ease. This isn't an inquisition. I see here that you seem to have met with Monsignor MacMerrigan's approval.
Moll	We got on great.
Fr Brest	And the new monsignor?
Moll	I couldn't tell you nothing about him father.
Fr Brest	Isn't it a wonder now you didn't stay on with him?
Moll	He didn't ask me father.
Fr Brest	And why not?
Moll	He brought his own woman with him father.
Fr Brest	You haven't worked for three months. Isn't that a long time to be without a job?
Moll	'Tis indeed father, a long time surely.
Fr Brest	Is it how you couldn't get a job?
Moll	I could get a job all right.
Fr Brest	And why didn't you take one?
Moll	After working nine years with a monsignor 'tisn't every job I *would* take. I couldn't bring myself to work with no less than a canon. 'Twould be a great come-down to me after all my years to have to fall into work with an ordinary priest.
Fr Brest	*(Looks to others for approval, laughs)* That's a very odd reason!
Canon Pratt	I don't know. I don't see anything odd about it.
Moll	'Tis hard canon, to come back to the plain black and

14

	white when one is used to the purple. Meaning no offence ….
Canon Pratt	No indeed. No indeed. And tell me now Miss Kettle, would you need help? What I mean is would you need an assistant?
Moll	An assistant canon?
Canon Pratt	A maidservant to help you.
Moll	I wouldn't leave one of 'em inside the door. A maidservant with curates in the house! We'll leave well enough alone canon.
Canon Pratt	How right you are Miss Kettle. What sort of a wage would you be expecting?
Moll	Eight pounds a week canon, and if we didn't fall out you might see your way to giving me a rise after a year or two.
Canon Pratt	I might so. I might so.
Fr Brest	Have you any hobbies?
Moll	Bingo father. Only on the Sunday night, and the television now and then.
Fr Brest	The disease of bingo: I see faith. Well we haven't been invaded by that particular malady in this parish yet and if I have my way we never will.
Fr Loran	Might I ask a question?
Canon Pratt	I suppose so.
Fr Loran	What do you think of Vatican Two?
Moll	What's that father?
Fr Loran	Vatican Two. What do you think of it?
Moll	Hawaii–Five–O is my own favourite father.
Canon Pratt	Now, now father. You mustn't expect the good woman to know about these things. Tell me Miss Kettle, when could you begin work … that is if we decided to take you on?
Moll	I could come in the morning canon.
Canon Pratt	I see. Well lads, any more questions?
Fr Brest	I presume Monsignor MacMerrigan had curates.
Moll	He had father, three of 'em.
Fr Brest	And did you get references from those?
Moll	I did not indeed.
Fr Brest	And why not?

Moll	No one takes notice of a curate's reference father.
Fr Brest	Huh?
Fr Loran	Nobody!
Moll	Well nobody except another curate.
	(The canon seems to enjoy this)
Fr Brest	No more questions.
Canon Pratt	Very well then. Miss Kettle would you be good enough to wait outside for a few minutes? I assure you we won't keep you long. *(Moll takes handbag, folds arms and exits. The canon rises and stands with his back to fireplace)* Now's the time to say it lads.
Fr Brest	I don't know ….
Canon Pratt	What don't you know?
Fr Brest	There's something about her.
Fr Loran	I think she's all right. She's not very bright but she's all right.
Fr Brest	*(Rises and paces)* Now that's where I disagree entirely with you. You say she's not very bright I say otherwise. She may give the impression that she's not bright but I say she's a lot sharper than she lets on to be.
Canon Pratt	And what if she is? So long as she fits the bill what else matters? I may tell you Phil, that I think we would be danged lucky to have her.
Fr Loran	I agree
Canon Pratt	Come on Phil, make it unanimous.
Fr Brest	I wish I could. This woman frightens me. There's something hidden beneath that calm surface. She's too quick with her answers.
Fr Loran	Now Phil …
Fr Brest	No Joe. I'm seriously concerned. When a presbytery gets a new housekeeper it's like a regiment that gets a new sergeant major. A new housekeeper is like a new moon and a new moon can bring anything from a tidal wave to an earthquake.
Canon Pratt	You're an alarmist Phil.
Fr Brest	Maybe but I have a foreboding. In these matters I'm as sensitive as a seismograph.
Fr Loran	A what?
Fr Brest	Seismograph!

Fr Loran	Oh, yes.
Fr Brest	And already I am recording the first faint vibrations of a calamity that is about to befall. I am registering the first awful rumblings of a collapsing presbytery. *(Others laugh, Fr Brest sits)*
Canon Pratt	Spare the flowery language for Sunday's sermon father.
Fr Brest	All right but don't forget I warned you.
Canon Pratt	Are we agreed then?
Others	Agreed.
Canon Pratt	I'm glad that we're decided. I think we chose wisely. *(Canon moves to the door)* Miss Kettle, will you come in please? *(Moll enters)* Will you be good enough to take a seat Miss Kettle? *(Moll sits)* Your Christian name is Maureen, is it not?
Moll	That's right canon although them that knows me calls me 'Moll'.
Canon Pratt	'Moll' is it? Well now Moll, we have good news for you girl. Whenever you're ready you can begin work. The salary is agreed. I'm sorry it's not more but we are a very poor parish with a new school to be built and repairs to the church and God knows what else.
Moll	'Tis all right canon. I'm sure I'll manage – as I've always done.
Canon Pratt	I dare say we might agree that a month's notice either way would be reasonable, in case things don't work out.
Moll	Ah, they'll work out fine canon, you'll see.
Canon Pratt	Very well then. If you'll come with me I'll show you the layout of the place *(Canon rises and indicates other exit. Moll rises)*
Moll	*(To all)* I hope now please God that it will be the lucky day for all of us.
Canon Pratt	Yes, please God.
Fr Loran	Please God.
Canon Pratt	Of course we have a handy man and then there's the parish clerk and as you say … *(Exit Moll and canon)*
Fr Loran	For better or for worse we have ourselves a housekeeper. *(Collects papers)*
Fr Brest	I've said my piece. Only time can tell. I hope for your

17

	sake and mine I'm proved wrong.
Fr Loran	I think you're being ridiculous, now, you know. *(Crosses to fireplace, puts papers away on top of pouffe there)*
Fr Brest	Remember that I am a veteran of five presbyteries and I happen to know that God's greatest blessing is a good housekeeper but that God's greatest curse is a bad one. I haven't met a bad one yet but I know men who have. They died from malnutrition. This woman strikes me as a bad one. I could be wrong but I feel it in my bones and my bones have yet to let me down. I have to go. I'll see you later. *(Moves to door down left)*
Fr Loran	Where are you going?
Fr Brest	I'm going for a round of golf if you must know but first I'm going out to the chapel and in the chapel I propose to go down on my two knees and commence a novena for the salvation of all of us, not to any saint and not to any martyr but straight through, no messing and no diversions, straight through to God the Father Almighty Himself. Be seein' you.
	(Exits)

Canon Pratt	Of the many afflictions that annoy the human condition the poisonous canker of Doubt seems to me one of the most potent and least recognised. And Doubt has an insidious and deadly effect upon the infected person bringing torment to the soul and encouraging a terrible railing against the will of God, erupting in fits of rage.
	For my part I thank God for the blessing of Optimism. And my faith in Optimism was never better justified than in the case of Moll Kettle for when I offered the opinion that we had chosen wisely in appointing her as our housekeeper my words were clearly divinely inspired …

Action takes place as before. The time is morning, a month later. The priests and canon are seated at table breakfasting. The canon is eating heartily, Fr Loran not so heartily and Fr Brest not at all. Moll enters with bowl of black and white pudding.

Moll	Excuse me canon. *(Loads canon's plate)*
Canon Pratt	Watch out, I'll burst.
Moll	Just a little more. Is the breakfast all right canon?
Canon Pratt	Fine, fine, couldn't be better. How long are you with us now Moll?
Moll	A month yesterday canon.
Canon Pratt	*(Heartily)* A month yesterday, faith. Well, now does time be long in passing? Off with you Moll. We're fine here.
Moll	Thank you canon. *(Is about to exit)* What about the dinner canon?
Canon Pratt	We'll leave that entirely to yourself Moll.
Moll	Would bacon and turnips be all right then?
Canon Pratt	Bacon and turnips would be glorious Moll, just glorious.
Moll	Thank you canon. *(Exits)*
Canon Pratt	There's a great woman.

19

Fr Brest	I don't know all about that.
Canon Pratt	*(Still eating away heartily)* You haven't hit it off with her Phil, have you?
Fr Brest	Quite frankly, no.
Canon Pratt	Well we mustn't let it spoil our breakfast.
	(Canon resumes eating. Fr Loran nibbles. Fr Brest does not eat but with his knife probes through objects on his plate. He frowns. He bends over plate, exaggeratedly peering at contents, finally he lifts up a tiny object. He holds it in front of him)
Fr Brest	Fr Loran?
Fr Loran	Yes Fr Brest.
Fr Brest	You're a man who has excellent eye-sight.
Fr Loran	Well, I don't need spectacles anyway, thanks be to God.
Fr Brest	That's good. Perhaps you could tell me what this is which I am holding in my hand. Take your time now … *(Fr Loran looks carefully at object and shakes his head)*
Fr Loran	It beats me.
Fr Brest	Does it remind you of anything?
Fr Loran	Offhand I can't say.
Fr Brest	Here take it in your hand and make a careful examination. *(Fr Loran accepts object and turns it over in his hand)* Interesting, isn't it?
Fr Loran	It certainly is. I must confess I'm baffled. *(Holds it out in front of him)* I honestly can't say what it is.
Fr Brest	Have you ever seen anything like it before?
Fr Loran	*(More examination)* N … No. I can't say that I have.
Fr Brest	Hand it back, please. It could be valuable.
Fr Loran	Valuable?
Fr Brest	Museums and universities are always interested in curiosities.
Canon Pratt	*(Crossly)* Do I detect a note of sarcasm Fr Brest, because if I do I may tell you here and now I won't have it. What in blazes are you on about then?
Fr Brest	*(Exhibits rasher)* It's this.
Canon Pratt	*(Suspiciously)* What is it?
Fr Brest	I wish I knew.
	(The canon peers closely at it)
Canon Pratt	Damn and blast it man, that's a rasher.

Fr Brest	Is it?
Canon Pratt	It is of course.
Fr Brest	But it's too small to be a rasher.
Canon Pratt	It's still a rasher.
Fr Brest	*(Irked)* It must have come off a bloody banbh.
Fr Loran	Or a pyg … my.
Canon Pratt	What?
Fr Loran	Get it, a pygmy, hah?
Canon Pratt	*(Conciliatory)* Come on Phil. Stop the nonsense and eat your breakfast, like a good boy.
Fr Brest	What breakfast?
Canon Pratt	The breakfast on your plate. I see nothing wrong with it.
Fr Brest	What you mean is there's nothing wrong with yours. You did all right for yourself. Look at the size of your sausages and look at the size of ours. *(He holds up a sausage)* What do you think of that?
Fr Loran	Normal sausages run about sixteen to the pound. Forty-eight of these wouldn't make a pound. Of course I don't mind. I haven't much of an appetite anyway but it's tough on poor Phil canon.
Fr Brest	You're bloody sure it's tough on poor Phil.
Canon Pratt	Maybe they are what are known as cocktail sausages. It's a fact you know that there could be more nourishment in a small meaty, hardy sort of a sausage than you'd get out of a big, fat, soft one.
Fr Brest	*(Sarcastically)* Is that a fact?
Canon Pratt	Oh, yes indeed. Isn't there a saying to cover it, what in blazes is it again … something to do with parcels.
Fr Loran	The best of goods come in small parcels.
Canon Pratt	That's the one. Good man Joe. There's a lot to some of these old sayings, you know.
Fr Brest	Fair enough then I'll tell you what we'll do. In future you can have the small hardy sausages and I'll take the big, fat ones.
Canon Pratt	What's gotten into you lately Phil?
Fr Brest	It's the housekeeper, your precious Moll. She seems to think the curates can live on the wind.
Canon Pratt	Now, now the poor woman does the best she can.

21

Fr Brest	She does the best she can for you.
Canon Pratt	That's your imagination.
Fr Brest	Is it …? *(Sticks a fork in the canon's remaining sausage. Sticks fork in one of his own sausages)* Have a look canon. Now is it my imagination? Am I seeing things canon, or is one of those sausages three times as large as the other? Am I seeing things Fr Loran?
Fr Loran	You are *not*.
Fr Brest	Am I canon …?
Canon Pratt	If you want fat sausages why in blazes don't you ask for fat sausages?
Fr Brest	*(Returning sausages)* All right, I'm asking for them now.
Canon Pratt	*(Coldly)* Very good. You've made your point. May we proceed with our breakfasts?
Fr Brest	You proceed by all means but I have something more to say.
Canon Pratt	*(Eating calmly)* You'd better get it off your chest then, hadn't you?
Fr Brest	Yes. I had better hadn't I? *(Fr Brest rises. Fr Loran would caution him to use restraint but Brest has the floor)* That woman in there, that so-called housekeeper has deliberately gone out of her way to make my life a misery since she came here a month ago. I was an easy-going placid man, a happy man in a happy house, content with my fare and with my lot and then slowly, insidiously, poisonously she tries to break me …
Canon Pratt	What a vivid imagination you have Phil.
Fr Brest	Have I? Have you heard her when she calls me? I'm relaxed and happy and then suddenly in the distance I hear the shriek … *(Imitates shrill, shrieking voice)* 'Fr Brest, Fr Breest', I tell you I'm shattered.
Canon Pratt	For God's sake Phil, gather hold of yourself. The poor woman has nothing against you.
Fr Brest	Hasn't she? Did I hear you agree to bacon and turnips for lunch today …?
Canon Pratt	Yes … but we can always change it if you want to …
Fr Brest	I know what I'll get today. I'll get the stringiest, toughest, smallest piece of the whole lot. Something leathery and lardy from the middle of an old sow's belly.

Fr Loran	So will I.
Fr Brest	*(To Loran angrily)* Yes, but you have no appetite and I have. *(To canon)* You watch it now at lunchtime … just see for yourself if I'm exaggerating … in the interests of common justice have a look at my plate.
Canon Pratt	Why don't you have a talk with her?
Fr Brest	I would never demean myself by talking with a creature like that.
Canon Pratt	Oh, dear me, we're very perturbed this morning.
Fr Brest	*(Spreading hands out for calm and reasoning)* All right. You remember yesterday's lunch?
Canon Pratt	*(Reluctantly)* Yes.
Fr Brest	What did it consist of?
Canon Pratt	I have an atrocious memory.
Fr Brest	I'll help you. Were there some lamb chops?
Canon Pratt	I believe there were some lamb chops.
Fr Brest	The exact number canon?
Canon Pratt	I think there were three.
Fr Brest	So there were three. Good. May I ask what else was on the plate?
Canon Pratt	*(Thoughtfully)* Peas I believe. Yes, I'm certain there were some peas.
Fr Brest	How many peas?
Canon Pratt	*(Laughs)* Oh, now Phil, I didn't count them …
Fr Brest	Of course you didn't. As I recall you had a very large plate. In fact I would not be wrong if I said that it was more of a dish than a plate …
Canon Pratt	*(Irritation)* Go on. Go on.
Fr Brest	Half the dish was taken up by the three lamb cutlets. What my dear canon, took up the rest of the area of the plate?
Canon Pratt	*(Sighs)* Peas I said but what's the point father?
Fr Brest	So we may presume that an area of almost one square foot was entirely covered by peas. How many peas would you say there were in this area of the plate?
Canon Pratt	*(Severely)* All right, there were a few hundred peas or thereabouts. I can't be certain.
Fr Brest	Thank you canon. You have been most helpful. Now did you see what was on my plate canon?

Canon Pratt	No. I did not. I had something better to do.
Fr Brest	Oh begob, you had! What was on my plate Fr Loran? And please speak up. *(Loran tries to speak but Brest flows on)* I want you to be heard. Now what was on my plate father?
Fr Loran	*(Entering into the spirit of the thing)* There was what appeared to be one small mutton chop or some article which outwardly resembled a small mutton chop. It was, if I may say so, the smallest mutton chop I have ever seen …
Fr Brest	Go on please. What else father?
Fr Loran	There also appeared to be a small quantity of what seemed to me to be tinned peas.
Fr Brest	Could we be a little bit more specific father? Take your time but be honest in your answer.
Fr Loran	It is my honest opinion that there were twenty peas on the plate.
Fr Brest	You are wrong father. I counted those peas and instead of twenty there were nineteen peas. Is this fair canon? Is this honest canon?
Canon Pratt	I'll talk to her. I had no hand in it I assure you. I'll talk to her this very day.
Fr Brest	I believe you but before I close let me add that I could not chew the meat of that chop yesterday. I tried and failed. I hacked at it and I tore at it but I made no impression. I can only conclude that the same chop which I euphemistically called mutton was not mutton at all. *(Goes furiously towards exit where he stands)* I can only conclude that it was hacked, gartered and hewn from the posterior of a mountain ram who was siring ewes when Holy St Patrick was a boy in the mountains of Antrim. *(Exits)*
Canon Pratt	By the Lord but that was a mighty outburst Joe.
Fr Loran	He's been complaining with a bit.
Canon Pratt	That's the first I heard.
Fr Loran	I suppose he kept it in for too long, hence the unexpected explosion.
Canon Pratt	And do you agree with him?
Fr Loran	Well, I do and I don't.

Canon Pratt	Well, do you or don't you?
Fr Loran	Well, I think I do but on the other hand ….
Canon Pratt	I'll have a talk with her.
	(In the distance can be heard the high pitched sound of Moll's voice calling Fr Brest)
Fr Loran	No time like the present. Here she comes. I'll skedaddle. *(Enter Moll)*
Moll	Where's Fr Brest?
Canon Pratt	Who wants him?
Moll	There's a sick call.
Fr Loran	I'll take it Miss Kettle.
Moll	Very well. The man is waiting outside.
Fr Loran	The ball is at your feet canon. Watch how you kick. *(Exits)*
Canon Pratt	Moll will you sit down for a minute? I want to have a little talk with you.
Moll	Very good canon. *(Moll takes a seat)*
Canon Pratt	Moll … poor Fr Brest is very perturbed.
Moll	Oh the poor man, I hope he'll get out of it!
Canon Pratt	He thinks you're cutting down on his food. So does Fr Loran but Loran doesn't seem to mind.
Moll	Enough is enough canon and I've always given the pair of them enough. Maybe 'tis how they expect the same as yourself.
Canon Pratt	That's just it Moll. They do and they have every right to expect it.
Moll	Have they no respect for seniority?
Canon Pratt	All I know is that Fr Brest maintains he is not getting enough to eat. Now what have you to say to that?
Moll	Your last housekeeper canon, spent forty pounds a month on meat alone for this household. That much money would keep a company of soldiers in meat. Forty pounds on meat alone.
Canon Pratt	Was it that much?
Moll	Every penny of it canon.
Canon Pratt	And how much was it this month Moll?
Moll	Ten pounds canon.
Canon Pratt	Great God Moll but you're a pure magician. And the food was never better. *(Corrects himself)* My food was

25

	never better. And did you cut down much on the other items Moll?
Moll	I did indeed canon. The grocery bill is cut by half.
Canon Pratt	Great God but you're a genius entirely Moll. Still we have this problem about Fr Brest.
Moll	God save us all canon but 'tis wrong to give young priests too much to eat.
Canon Pratt	Why would you say that Moll?
Moll	Because they gets notions canon.
Canon Pratt	Notions Moll?
Moll	Notions canon. Over in Scotland canon a few years ago a young curate rose up one morning without his collar and went off with a half-naked lady acrobat.
Canon Pratt	Ah, go on …
Moll	A lady acrobat. 'Twas in the papers canon. Beef canon, and steaks that was half raw was the cause of it. That was what Monsignor MacMerrigan's doctor told us. He knew the curate. If 'twas plain bread and butter and gravy he was getting he'd be too weak to get notions.
Canon Pratt	I dare say there's something in what you say Moll.
Moll	In the name of God canon, will you look at the jaunty cut of them two hardy bucks.
Canon Pratt	Ah, now they're young and they're …
Moll	Isn't that what I'm at canon?
Canon Pratt	Huh?
Moll	Two prime bucks and they have the gall to look for more food. Sure if they eat any more they'll go out of their minds altogether. If you feed them like game-cocks they'll crow like gamecocks and they'll strut like gamecocks.
Canon Pratt	And you think they're getting enough?
Moll	Are they priests or are they gluttons canon? Is there nothing else to life but their gullets? Would you hear the pope asking for lamb cutlets? When Cardinal Monsooki from Persia came to see the monsignor two years ago, did he ask for lamb cutlets? He did not indeed. A plate of giblet soup and a crust of bread was all the poor man had and he a cardinal. Yet we have two pampered bucks looking for lamb cutlets, begrudging

	their own canon the bite he does be eating. What worries have them two beyond the filling of their bellies? Have they to think about the education of children and the building of schools or is their guts their only concern?
Canon Pratt	I can't answer you Moll. In all truth Moll, I can't answer you.
Moll	*(She rises and starts to tidy table)* And will you tell me another thing canon?
Canon Pratt	I will if I can Moll.
Moll	The church canon. There's three holes in the roof, canon, and the windows are rotten. Are the people of the parish canon, to be exposed to rain and cold and draughts because Fr Brest don't like bingo?
Canon Pratt	The people of the parish must come before all else Moll, before me, you, before anybody.
Moll	Would you like to see the old people catching pneumonia when they kneel down to say their prayers? Is that what you want canon? Is it how you want the feeble and the delicate to be bent over with pain, and them that has weak joints to be crippled?
Canon Pratt	'Tis not what I want Moll.
Moll	We'll be all racked with pleurisy and T.B. if them holes in the roof aren't seen to. And why canon? Will you tell me why?
Canon Pratt	Because Fr Brest doesn't like bingo.
Moll	And does he like bridge canon?
Canon Pratt	By all accounts he's a dab hand at it Moll.
Moll	And golf canon. Don't he play golf?
Canon Pratt	He plays golf. In fact he has won tournaments Moll.
Moll	So 'tis all right for Fr Brest and his equals to play golf and bridge.
Canon Pratt	Yes. 'Tis all right for them.
Moll	*(About to exit with hands full of breakfast things)* But 'tis not all right for the poor people of this parish to play an innocent game of bingo.
	(Enter Brest in a hurry)
Fr Brest	Well did you have a talk with Moll about the food?
Canon Pratt	Indeed I did – we're putting a new roof on the church.
Fr Brest	What's that got to do with it – where are you going to

get the money?

Canon Pratt   *You're* going to get it Fr Brest. From now on you're in charge of the bingo.
(Moll laughs and exits)

Canon Pratt   If there is a sound that pleases me more than most 'tis the sound of laughter. Laughter erupts from the soul in an irrepressible declamation of an excess of good humour.

    Laughter is natural, you see. 'Tis one of the many magical gifts the good Lord provides. The warmth of the sun, the whisper of the trees, the murmur of the sea. The nectar of the very air we breathe. Go right ahead, says the Lord. 'Tis free. Enjoy it.

The time is evening of a day several months after the arrival of Moll Kettle. Moll is dusting. As she dusts the several chairs they bring to her mind her impressions of the three who normally sit in them. Then she goes to dust a picture behind the door down left and while she is there the two curates burst in, concealing her behind it.

Fr Brest   We made it. *(Shakes Loran's hand)* Congratulations *(Loran puzzled)* on evading you know who. I'll ring the mother while I have the chance. She's taken to listening in on telephone calls now. *(Picks up the phone to dial)* The other night I was on to her and in the middle of the conversation I sensed there was someone in the vicinity. *(Puts down phone)*

Fr Loran   And was she there?

Fr Brest   She was standing behind the door of this very room. *(With his back to it slams the door. Loran sees Moll, but Brest doesn't)* Still as a statue, hardly breathing, with an innocent look on her face as if she weren't listening at all. *(Loran gestures, Brest turns and sees Moll)* What are you doing there?

Moll   Doing where boybawn?

Fr Brest   Doing there; hiding behind the door.

Moll   Cobwebs, I'm hunting cobwebs. The presbytery is draped with them.

Fr Brest   Do you realise that I was making a phone call to my

	mother? You were eavesdropping again, you ought to be ashamed of yourself. Would you mind leaving the room now so that I can ring my mother?
Moll	I'll go boybawn when I have the cobwebs cleared.
Fr Brest	You'll go now!
Moll	I was here before you.
Fr Brest	If you don't leave this room instantly I will remove you forcibly.
Fr Loran	Keep your temper! No violence.
Moll	I'm going to say a rosary for the poor souls – but remember one thing …
Fr Brest	What would that be?
Moll	A call to your mother is not church business.
Fr Brest	Meaning what?
Moll	Meaning that you can leave the money for the call beside the phone. *(She exits in triumph)*
Fr Loran	Well, mother love is a wonderful thing – but it will cost you money from now on.
Fr Brest	May God forgive me but I can't bear that woman. *(On phone)* Get me Castletownbere 49.
Fr Loran	*(Putting his coat and hat on small table up-stage)* We are supposed to show meekness and sufferance in the face of adversity. Our first function is forbearance.
Fr Brest	It's me or she and by the Lord Heavens it's not going to be me … no, no miss, not you … I mean it's going to be me or she … all right, ring me back *(Puts down phone)*
Fr Loran	Well, what was it you were going to tell me?
Fr Brest	*(Tossing down a letter)* What do you think of that?
Fr Loran	What is it?
Fr Brest	Take a look.
Fr Loran	*(Reluctantly takes out the letter)* You wrote to Monsignor MacMerrigan!
Fr Brest	I did.
Fr Loran	*(Reading)* He's in rare form all right … 'let me say that you have an irrational impertinence which will land you in hot water some day. So you want further information about Moll Kettle. If you must know she was a great woman entirely. She ran the presbytery on a pittance and if there were more like her there wouldn't be

half the trouble in the Church today. You are an impatient and ungodly fellow to want to belittle this woman. Prayer is the last hope for you, prayer and meditation. I need not add fasting because Moll Kettle will see to that. Ha. Ha. May God succour you father and your many Godless equals. The Church is at the crossroads. Make sure you follow the right path. Yours in J. C. Monsignor Patrick MacMerrigan.' *(Returns the letter)*

Fr Brest How did an old bags like that come to be a monsignor?

Fr Loran Probably fit for nothing else.

Fr Brest I also wrote to two of his curates.

Fr Loran I thought there were three.

Fr Brest There were but one died shortly after Moll left.

Fr Loran From what?

Fr Brest From a mixture of maleficence, malnutrition and pernicious anaemia.

Fr Loran That last one. What is it?

Fr Brest It's what you and I will die from if we don't get to her first.

Fr Loran That's nice. Did you get replies to those letters?

Fr Brest I did.

Fr Loran Show us. *(Brest is about to hand over both, but on second thoughts retains one and reads it out himself)*

Fr Brest This is from Fr Paddy O'Shaughnessy who was the senior curate in Moll's early time with MacMerrigan. *(Reads)* 'Dear Phil, Good to hear from you. Saw where you won the West Cork fourball. Congrats. I heard a great night was had by all and you had to be carried … *(Brest stops and edits the next section of the letter)* About our friend to whom I will not refer by name as I would put nothing past her, not even the steaming open of this letter…'

Fr Loran I don't doubt him. I don't doubt him one bit.

Fr Brest Quiet … *(Reads)* 'I am, as you know from our student days, a more than passable linguist. In point of fact I now speak four languages fluently. I have a fair knowledge of seven others but in the entire eleven there is no word or group of words which would adequately describe the demon in your midst. Cunning, sharp, deadly, evil itself personified. In the early days of the human species before language was needed she would have been eliminated by what bookmakers refer to as tick-tack. My current choice of foods is grossly restricted from the beating she gave my stomach. You know me Phil. We got on, you and I, but lest there be any doubt in your mind about you know who remember Fr Paul Mannick, our dear departed colleague.'

Fr Loran	Is that the third one?
Fr Brest	Yes.
Fr Loran	Requiescat in Pace.
Fr Brest	'If he could shed the boards and the brown cloths that bind him and rise from the grave he would point a bony finger in the direction of a certain woman whose name is known to all of us. I conclude. Yours fondly, Fr Paddy O'Shaughnessy. P.S. In the honour of God either burn or ate this epistle.'
Fr Loran	Cogent.
Fr Brest	Most cogent.
Fr Loran	Tells its own tale.
Fr Brest	Forcibly.
Fr Loran	Agreed.
Fr Brest	*(Proudly)* However that last letter from the middle curate as he styles himself, tells all succinctly and savagely.
Fr Loran	*(Reading)* 'Dear Fr Brest, I am only the middle curate. You should not involve me. I am neither craven nor cowardly but remember that she who is your housekeeper today could be mine tomorrow. *(Look of alarm at Brest)* For this reason, I am afraid to say more but I'll put it this way. If I were sending a telegram it would say "abandon ship". Sincerely, Robert Connors, C.C.' *(Returns letter)*
Fr Brest	Paints a strange picture, does it not?
Fr Loran	Weird. What are we going to do?
Fr Brest	There's only one thing we can do.
Fr Loran	What's that?
Fr Brest	The bishop.
Fr Loran	You mean a visit?

Fr Brest	Not necessarily, a confidential letter would do.
Fr Loran	That's pretty drastic.
Fr Brest	She's been with us four months and already I have conducted fifty sessions of bingo, each lasting four hours. I have lost fifteen pounds in weight. I have become a martyr to malnutrition. It will have to be the bishop. A joint letter.
Fr Loran	Count me out.
Fr Brest	You can't opt out. We have to make a stand.
Fr Loran	It won't work.
Fr Brest	Why not?
Fr Loran	Because once you've written one letter to the bishop you can never do it again. Suppose we write to him and tell him the truth about Moll, we will forever after, in his eyes, be the two curates who complained about the food. If sometime either one of us has another complaint to make, he'll say to himself that is one of the two who complained before. You get it?
Fr Brest	No. I don't get it. We have a genuine grouse.
Fr Loran	But have we? There's plenty bread and butter. There's milk and there are potatoes. No scarcity of essentials if you know what I mean. If the bishop investigates he's not going to do so without informing the canon and informing the canon, as we both know, is the same as informing Moll. She'll be ready for the bishop. Is it a woman that fobbed off Cardinal Monsooki with watery giblet soup?
Fr Brest	You won't sign then?
Fr Loran	Let's wait. If things get worse I'll reconsider. We have very little to show you know; we have no proof. Honestly, Phil, you may have lost weight but you were overeating. You've never looked as fit. Your belly's gone. You're not flabby anymore.
Fr Brest	I'm living off my fat, I tell you, and when that runs out it's only a matter of time until the major collapse. Hush … *(To door)* what was that? *(Both men become alert and listen carefully. Brest opens door slightly, Loran comes up behind him. Both listen, Brest turns)*
Fr Loran	It sounds like the banshee to me.

Fr Brest	Worse. It's the voice of Moll Kettle. Listen ….
	(Again they both listen and after a little while unmistakably Moll's voice can be heard)
Moll	Fr Breest … where are you? … Fr Breest.
Fr Brest	There's no escape. *(Produces letters)* Let's burn this lot. *(He opens and crumbles them, helped by Fr Loran. They light the pile)*
Fr Loran	Give them to me and I'll burn them. *(At fireplace)* Here she is. *(Enter Moll)*
Moll	Fr Bree … Oh, there you are!
Fr Brest	What's the matter now?
Moll	The matter is that there's a sick call and there's no priest to take it.
Fr Brest	We're off-duty.
Moll	One of you is supposed to be on call.
Fr Brest	The canon is also a priest, you know. He was ordained too, the same as Fr Loran and myself.
Moll	The canon went to bed an hour ago with a cold in the head and I have no notion of sending him traipsing into the countryside not knowing would he catch his death of pneumonia.
Fr Brest	Where is the sick call?
Moll	Hurry on. The man is waiting at the door of the presbytery. Hurry on before some poor soul faces his maker without a priest. *(Goes out door)*
Fr Brest	There's no peace to be had any more.
Moll	*(Comes back)* Wouldn't it be nice now if the bishop heard there was no priest to take a sick call? Suppose I didn't bother searching. 'Tis not my duty you know to locate missing curates. *(Goes out)*
Fr Brest	That will do you now. Enough guff, thank you.
Moll	*(Comes back)* What's the bonfire for?
Fr Loran	Just some waste Miss Kettle. 'Tis all right.
Fr Brest	I don't see that it's any of your business.
Moll	Waste paper that had to be burned. Ha! Ha! That must have been the hot paper.
Fr Brest	If it wasn't hot before it's hot now.
Moll	*(About to exit)* You'd better hurry and don't forget the two of you are on the bingo tonight in the parish hall.

Fr Brest	Tonight is Wednesday – there's no bingo.
Moll	There's a special session tonight for the Church holiday.
Fr Brest	And I was playing golf with the doctor.
Fr Loran	And I was playing records for the reverend mother …
Moll	Well now, legs eleven, the doc can go play golf with the reverend mother; because tonight the pair of you are on the bingo. Check!
	(Exits)

Canon Pratt A word about the bingo. Bingo is no sin. There are some who will tell you that bingo is gambling and that therefore bingo is a pernicious evil preying upon the vulnerability of simple people.

Yirra, bingo is not gambling at all but a harmless bit o' fun. The prizes are modest and, though welcome, unlikely to launch a winner into the perilous seas of high finance, particularly since there is every encouragement to reinvest in the parish funds for the glorification of God and the salvation of the donor's soul.

Moll at the telephone.

Moll *(On phone)* There's none of the curates here now. *(Listens)* Oh! The canon is resting and can't be disturbed … *(Listens)* You must talk to him … a matter of life and death? Listen here to me now. Fr Loran is at choir practice. Fr Brest is in bed. I'm not going to call the canon unless there's anointing to be done. What's up with you anyway? *(Listens)* You're pregnant? Well that's hardly the fault of the canon. *(Listens)* Yes? Yes? You had a right to think of that my dear girl before you let him put the honey in your coffee. *(Listens)* A what? He gave you a green cough drop and told you 'twas the pill. You must be a right eejit. *(Puts down the phone)*

Bridgie *(Coming in)* 'Tis me. The canon isn't in, I suppose, is he? I suppose he isn't, is he?

Moll Weren't you one of the women in for this job?

Bridgie That's right. No hard feelings.

Moll What can I do for you?

Bridgie *(Sits down)* I want to see one of the curates.

Moll They're not here now.

Bridgie *(Sits left of table)* The canon will do just as well.

Moll The canon is resting.

Bridgie Oh dear! That's a pity.

Moll Maybe I might be able to help. I often stands in for the

	canon. Out with it now, whatever it is.
Bridgie	I'm thinking of getting married.
Moll	Are you in earnest?
Bridgie	Oh, I am!
Moll	And who is he?
Bridgie	*(Calls)* Ulick … Ulick love … come in and let the woman see you … *(Enter a man of advanced years, wearing a cap and long overcoat. He is the very epitome of deference. He wears strong-lensed specs)* He's very shy.
Moll	Will you sit down sir? *(He smiles and shrugs his way out of doing so)* Are you sure you want to go ahead?
Bridgie	What's wrong with him?
Moll	He'll die on the job.
Bridgie	If he do, won't I have my widow's pension!
Moll	What do you want to get married for anyway?
Bridgie	I have to.
Moll	You have to? Miracles will never cease. There's hope for us all. *(To Ulick)* Shove out here wonder-boy till I have a look at you.
Bridgie	Shove out Ulick, and let the woman have a look at you.
Moll	Are you sure he's the man?
Bridgie	He's the best I could get. I'm no chicken, you know.
Moll	Will you answer an honest question?
Bridgie	Of course.
Moll	Are you long gone?
Bridgie	Long gone where?
Moll	You know where.
Bridgie	I don't, honest I don't.
Moll	How many months?
Bridgie	What are you talking about?
Moll	You said you had to get married.
Bridgie	*(Goes into paroxysm of laughter)* Did you hear that Ulick? What she's pinning on you? Yirra get on with ya. I have to get married because I can't get a job. I spent my life working for priests and here I am penniless in the end.
Moll	God knows 'tis true. And did you save anything?
Bridgie	Save on what a priest would pay? You must be mad. The same thing will happen to you some day unless you look out for yourself.

Moll	*(Thoughtfully)* There's a lot to what you say. You've put me thinking, God knows.
Bridgie	How much to get married anyway?
Moll	Two pounds a cow, ten shillings a bullock, five bob a sheep, two bob a goat and a shilling a pig.
Bridgie	How many cows have you Ulick? *(Ulick lifts four fingers of left hand and holds up other hand clenched)* Four cows and a bull.
Moll	Eight pounds. Yerra give me a forty quid and I'll come round the canon. You gave me good advice. If I don't look out for myself the canon won't.
Bridgie	Have you forty handy Ulick? *(Ulick locates purse and extracts money, Bridgie takes it and hands it to Moll, who accepts it)*
Moll	Let the two of you be here next Monday morning at eight o'clock. *(Moll listens to noise outside)* Go on now. Off ye go.
Bridgie	I'll be looking forward to it, and pray that I'll be guided right. *(Exit Bridgie)*
Moll	Ulick? *(Ulick pauses)* Take it nice and easy at the start. If you get over the first fence without a fall you'll finish the course no bother.
Ulick	There's no fear of a fall. I'd say she was often saddled before. *(Exit Ulick)*

END OF ACT ONE

ACT TWO

SCENE ONE

Action takes place in the dining cum sitting-room of the presbytery. The canon is sitting in a comfortable chair near the fire, while Moll arranges table for supper. The canon smokes his pipe. In the distance can be heard the voices of men and women singing the Adoremus …

Moll	I can put up the supper any time canon.
Canon Pratt	We'll wait Moll, till Fr Loran is finished with the choir practice. That was a great idea of yours to get a choir going.
Moll	Thank you canon.
Canon Pratt	Do you like hymns Moll?
Moll	I do canon, but hymns are sad.
Canon Pratt	That's just the way Fr Loran's choir sings them. How long are you here now Moll?
Moll	*(Laying table)* Gone the twelve months canon.
Canon Pratt	Gone the twelve months. That bingo was a great idea too. The bare year gone by and the church is repaired, the foundations for the school are dug and work will start next week. I never thought I'd live to see the day. The bishop is your happy man. Did I tell you he complimented me on the fundraising?
Moll	Did he now?
Canon Pratt	He told me I was a credit to the diocese. I'm very mindful, said he, of good builders and I'm very thankful, said he, to priests who build modern schools. I often think of them, he said.
Moll	*(Repeats)* He often think of them. What did he mean by that, I wonder?
Canon Pratt	You never know till after what a bishop means Moll, as many a poor priest knows to his cost. All we can do is hope for the best. Still and all, the outlook is good and God is good too.
Moll	God knows but 'tis fine for you. 'Tis how you'll wind up bishop one day yourself.
Canon Pratt	Doubtful Moll, but men were made monsignors with

	far less to their credit.
Moll	'Tis fine for some.
Canon Pratt	*(Looks at her suspiciously)* Am I right in thinking we have a touch of the sulks today …? Come on Moll. You know me. Out with it, whatever it is.
Moll	I don't know should I canon.
Canon Pratt	Sit down Moll. *(Moll takes a seat)* Now let's have it. 'Tis always better to get a thing out. And you know me … It won't pass my lips whatever it is. You may talk to me in complete confidence.
Moll	'Tis money canon.
Canon Pratt	There are other things in the world besides money girl. There is the grace of God which is more important than all the wealth and all the riches of the five continents put together.
Moll	True for you canon but couldn't a person have the grace of God and have a bit of money beside it?
Canon Pratt	Spell it out to me Moll.
Moll	I won't put a tooth in it canon. Security, my own security has me worried sick. I'm getting old canon and you're not getting any younger yourself so 'tis time I thought about what I would do should anything happen to you. I'd be worse off than a widow.
Canon Pratt	Worse than a widow?
Moll	She would have her widow's pension. I wouldn't have a copper to get from anyone. It's not fair canon.
Canon Pratt	You shouldn't worry Moll. If anything happens to me you won't be forgotten. You'll get your severance pay. That will be seen to – and fifty pounds of a gift in my will to you.
Moll	Fifty pounds?
Canon Pratt	In black and white.
Moll	By God, you're a gas man with your fifty pounds – 'twould hardly buy a bicycle.
Canon Pratt	What would you say Moll, if I increased it to a hundred?
Moll	You can do the same with that as you did with the fifty – you'll have to do more.
Canon Pratt	Such as?

Moll	Such as a pension scheme and a bulk sum. Everyone gets them these days, and I'm as much entitled to them as the next person.
Canon Pratt	I've never heard the like! A bulk sum and a pension scheme? One would think you were a teacher or a higher civil servant.
Moll	If I were married to you wouldn't I have a life insurance on you? If I was your daughter wouldn't you have to give me a fortune?
Canon Pratt	We'll see, we'll see – a pension now is a different matter.
Moll	Them curates had a right hare made out of you before I came – you were up to your neck in debts and you were run off your feet. 'Twas me that done the worryin' and 'twas me that took charge of the bingo and the raffles. I would be expecting a pension of seven or eight pounds a week and a thousand pounds in a bulk sum.
Canon Pratt	A thousand pounds? Tell me 'tis a nightmare I'm having – where would I get a thousand pounds?
Moll	I'll show you how to make it … You can take my word for it canon, that there's a lot more in this parish than you'd think. There's them that lets on to be poor would buy and sell you. What are the people paying into Mass at present?
Canon Pratt	Two new pence.
Moll	*(Dismisses it)* That's nothing short of scandalous. Coppers for Mass, ten shillings for the dance hall. If Monsignor MacMerrigan was here he'd have 'em skinned while you'd be lookin' around you. He was a great warrant to gauge the amount of cash in a parish … and to get it out of 'em. The monsignor would never go to a pulpit. *(Imitating him)* 'I don't want to divorce myself from the people,' he used to say. 'The minute I go there Moll,' he used to say, 'I leave their world'. The monsignor knew all the tricks … He'd saunter out nice and easy, and lean back against the altar, like he'd be after meeting you in the street. Then he'd give the blessing, careless and gay and then he'd stick the two hands into the trouser pockets … *(Canon follows this and imitates all*

	the actions seriously) He had a fine, soft, deep voice; very oily and greasy … 'Well, well, well, well,' he'd say, 'here we are again. What's this I'm after taking out of my trousers pocket? Ah, it's a penny! I will give this penny to this lovely girl in the front seat – but wait a minute! What an old fool I am! A penny is no use to her. If she wanted to buy sweets or an apple or an ice cream a penny would be worthless. I had better give her a shilling … So now, in the honour of God, when you come to Mass next Sunday leave the pennies at home and bring a piece of silver with you. I'll be standing at the gate myself so don't blackguard me. I'm too old for it. I don't deserve it. Forget about today. We can all make mistakes. Just get this clear; I don't want to see anyone make a mistake on Sunday next. Remember, no coppers.' *(Turns up to right)*
Canon Pratt	Did it work?
Moll	Did it what! The following Sunday the Mass contributions were trebled, and it was the same every Sunday after that. Go on canon, give it a go yourself.
	(The canon steps forward and adopts the monsignor's pose. He begins confidently enough but soon degenerates into a mutter)
Canon Pratt	Well, well, well, well, here we are again. What's this I have in my trouser pocket? A penny, what have I in my other pocket? Why it's a shilling, five new pence. A penny in one hand and a shilling in the other. Um … *(He peters out)* We must go over it a few times.
Moll	Don't worry you'll have it right for Sunday. And another thing canon, them cards are a right money spinner.
Canon Pratt	Good Lord Moll, now you're not suggesting a poker school?
Moll	Not the playing cards – the Mass cards.
Canon Pratt	What about the Mass cards Moll?
Moll	I don't know where to start canon.
Canon Pratt	Start at the beginning Moll.
Moll	Fr Brest signed nine yesterday morning for the Mc-Goory funeral, while you were saying Mass. That's

	nine pounds.
Canon Pratt	Nine pounds in a morning. That's mighty money.
Moll	It should be your money canon.
Canon Pratt	He says the Masses Moll. He's entitled to the money.
Moll	Twelve times I had to answer the door for the pair of them. Most people wanting to get you to sign.
Canon Pratt	*(Thoughtfully)* That's twelve pounds between them.
Moll	And when you came back how many did you sign yourself canon?
Canon Pratt	Well now Moll, I didn't sign twelve anyway or anything near it, I may tell you.
Moll	That's what I thought canon.
Canon Pratt	*(Cutely)* And what would you recommend Moll?
Moll	'Tisn't for me to say canon.
Canon Pratt	Maybe not Moll but I may tell you I value your advice. You won't put me astray at any rate.
Moll	I'm only suggesting now, mind you.
Canon Pratt	I'm here for suggestions girl.
Moll	If you were to sign a big bundle of Mass cards and give them to me, I needn't be sending people away, saying you're not in or telling them to call back again. When I tell them you'll be back later they say Fr Brest will do or Fr Loran will do. That's honest money out of your pocket canon … honest money … You're losing hundreds canon … hundreds ….
Canon Pratt	*(Alarmed)* Hundreds! Faith, I suppose I am.
Moll	Hundreds canon. 'Tis not unnatural for a person to be fond of money canon … to want money in the pocket so that the house can be run and the parish can be run and all of us paid our wages. 'Tis you that pays them canon and 'tis no wonder you'd need money canon. 'Tisn't for yourself you want it.
Canon Pratt	'Tis not indeed.
Moll	'Tis no sin canon.
Canon Pratt	'Tis no sin Moll. So whoever would come to the door with money for a Mass card you would be there to meet them with the signed card.
Moll	'Tis me always answers the door canon.
Canon Pratt	'Tis a good idea God knows, but isn't there a danger

	Moll, that you would give my signed cards to those who would be seeking Fr Brest or Fr Loran?
Moll	I suppose it could happen all right canon. We all makes mistakes.
Canon Pratt	God help us but we do Moll. I'm sure you wouldn't do anything deliberate. You're not that sort as we all know well. *(Rubs chin)* The more I think of it the more I like it.
Moll	People set more store in a card signed by a canon than in a card signed by a curate.
Canon Pratt	I'll sign the cards first thing in the morning Moll.
Moll	*(Producing a bundle of cards)* Sure sign a few of them now canon, it will give you an appetite for your supper.
Canon Pratt	… and about our little problem …
Moll	We'll go to a solicitor and get him to draw up an agreement.
Canon Pratt	I make no promises, mind you, but allowing I could raise the thousand, I still think it's too much … We'll talk about it tomorrow.
Moll	I won't be here tomorrow morning! I'm shoving on. I'll go out in the world and find an old man that will marry me.
Canon Pratt	Moll!
Moll	An old man to marry me canon, and the older the better, because if the heart gives out on him I'll have my widow's pension, and that's a damn sight better than I'll ever see from you with your shining shoes and purple, and your grace of God.
Canon Pratt	The bishop would have to be consulted…
Moll	Will the bishop carry the breakfast up to bed to you tomorrow morning?
Canon Pratt	I'll see what can be done.
Moll	There's no seeing, you'll do it or you won't do it. If you do it I'll stay and if you don't do it I won't stay.
Canon Pratt	Be reasonable.
Moll	*(Collects duster, half goes)* I'll say goodbye to you before I go and pack my bags. All I can say is I hope you'll be lucky, and that you'll be minded half as well as I minded you. *(Sheds a tear)*
Canon Pratt	Wait! Wait a minute! Sit down, sit. It's bad to be hasty.

44

Moll	It is canon. You look after me, and I'll look after you. Look at the thousands I'll collect for you in Mass card money – sure there isn't a woman in Ireland would do as well by you.
Canon Pratt	All right, I'll do it, but you'll have to show me how. I haven't a penny, I swear it.
Moll	That's easy done. *(Stands)* Tomorrow we'll go to a solicitor and get him to draw up an agreement that whoever is parish priest after you must pay me the pension – that's important – and we'll go to the bank and raise the thousand. You'll have no bother. A parish priest's word is stronger than the Rock of Gibraltar. There's no bank manager in the world would refuse you. You put the thousand in your own name and mine with the proviso that if anything happens to you I claim it.
Canon Pratt	And if anything happens to you I can claim it.
Moll	Yes. Set yourself down there now and put your autograph on that bundle and I'll go fetch the supper. *(Moll goes to leave as the canon busies himself but on second thoughts she returns)* Er ... 'Tis a job you wouldn't expect me to do for nothing canon.
Canon Pratt	How's that Moll?
Moll	Giving out the cards and collecting the money for you ... There's a lot of responsibility.
Canon Pratt	I'm not sure I understand you.
Moll	A commission canon?
Canon Pratt	A commission would be totally unprecedented. I declare to God but I never heard the like.
Moll	You won't lose by it canon.
Canon Pratt	What sort of commission?
Moll	A shilling in the pound, sure 'tis only five new pence. 'Tisn't much.
Canon Pratt	Moll, it's totally unprecedented.
Moll	I used to get if from Monsignor Mac Merrigan.
Canon Pratt	In that case I see no reason why you shouldn't get it from me. Five pence in the pound it will be.
Moll	I'll go and get the supper now canon.
Canon Pratt	Will you give Fr Brest a call Moll?
Moll	I will to be sure canon and would you ever ask those

	two buckos to tidy out their rooms? They're in an awful state altogether.
Canon Pratt	And Moll?
Moll	Yes canon.
Canon Pratt	Call him easy. He says your voice is affecting his ear-drums.
Moll	I'll call him like he was a baby canon. He's a pure baba, God help us. *(Moll laughs and is joined by the canon. Exit Moll calling out at the top of her voice. Off)* Fr Breest … Fr Breest … your supper is on the table … *(Enter Fr Loran)*
Canon Pratt	And how's the choir going father?
Fr Loran	Did you ever spend two hours in a rookery canon?
Canon Pratt	Patience father, patience. We can't all be Carusos. These are simple people with no musical background. 'Tisn't a cathedral we have.
Fr Loran	Is it true you'll be getting a new organ for the church?
Canon Pratt	We'll have to ask Moll about that.
Fr Loran	Moll? Does she know something about organs?
Canon Pratt	I wouldn't say so but I'd say she knows something about the price of them.
Fr Loran	We'd badly want a new organ.
Canon Pratt	Why don't you talk to her yourself about it?
Fr Loran	I did.
Canon Pratt	And what did she say?
Fr Loran	She said I could have it if I had the price of it.
Canon Pratt	And have you the price of it?
Fr Loran	I haven't the price of a mouth organ.
Canon Pratt	I like it when a man bares his soul and says his piece.
Fr Loran	You do?
Canon Pratt	Of course.
Fr Loran	You like music don't you?
Canon Pratt	I like a good song and I like the fiddle played softly.
Fr Loran	That's not what I mean. What I mean is a massive choir drawn from the people of this parish. We don't have to confine ourselves to church music, you know.
Canon Pratt	You mean good rousing choruses like you'd hear in the pubs of a Saturday night.
Fr Loran	No. I do not. I mean one hundred men and one hun-

	dred women singing the Mass. Think of Schubert, think of Handel, think of the effect …
Canon Pratt	I don't know about Schubert, but you're off your handle all right. Do you think the people of this parish have nothing better to do?
Fr Loran	It could be done.
Canon Pratt	Choirs are all right for women that have their families reared or for young nuns that are in danger of deserting.
Fr Loran	We could give it a trial.
Canon Pratt	Sure … But wait till you have your own parish.
Fr Loran	When I have my own parish I'll have the greatest choir ever heard.
Canon Pratt	By the time you have your own parish you won't have the energy.
Fr Loran	*(Places hand across stomach)* By the Lord I'm hungry. Is she looking after the supper?
Canon Pratt	We were waiting on you. She's gone calling Fr Brest.
Fr Loran	Softly, I noticed.
Canon Pratt	Now, now there's no call for sarcasm. I don't know what's gotten into the pair of you this past year.
Fr Loran	I'm not prepared to discuss it canon. I'm too weak. Discussion might only weaken me further. I'll die young. You'll find me in my bed some morning with my tongue hanging out.
	(Enter Fr Brest. He seems older somehow and not as spruce as he was. His grooming is not what it was. He is bedraggled. When he enters he goes to fireplace where he elaborately extracts two gobs of cotton wool from his ears)
Fr Brest	I was upstairs resting from the fatigue of last night's bingo. Faintly, most melodiously in the distance, the gentle voices of Fr Loran's choristers sweetly assailed my ears. Ah, said I, this is sweet peace that cannot last. *(Laughs bitterly)* How right I was. Suddenly the awful shriek of Moll Kettle came to rend the silence apart. The birds were hushed. Time says I for my cotton wool.
Fr Loran	Does it soften the blow?
Fr Brest	Only a little. Nothing my dear father, is proof against the rasping screech of our dear housekeeper.

Canon Pratt	Ah! *(Enter Moll bearing plates)*
Moll	*(Loudly)* Was you asleep Fr Brest?
Fr Brest	Luckily! No.
Moll	And how is the eardrums this evening?
Fr Brest	*(Looks towards canon)* And pray who told you about my eardrums?
Moll	*(Putting down food)* Sure the whole parish knows about them. Come on the supper will be cold.
Fr Brest	And what array of delicacies are we to behold this evening?
Canon Pratt	*(Rising, rubbing his hands and taking his seat happily at table)* It's scrambled eggs on toast and it looks good. Come on lads, sit down. Fetch the tea Moll.
Moll	Here boybawn. Have a look at that while your havin' your supper.
Fr Brest	What is it?
Moll	'Tis a catalogue for the most up to date bingo ball dispensers. Turn to page fourteen and tell me what you see. *(Brest does so)* That bingo machine dispenses bingo balls of every hue. Black balls, blue balls, green balls, balls for every colour of the rainbow. *(Exits)*
	(Both curates seat themselves. The canon says grace and is answered by the curates. The canon immediately plunges into supper. Fr Brest produces a pair of glasses, dons them and inspects plate with great care)
Fr Brest	What a way for an innocent egg to end up. I'm glad I'm not the hen that laid it. *(Locates slice of bread and commences to butter it. He nibbles. Enter Moll with teapot. She rests it on the table. Fr Brest's eyes are glued to his plate)*
Moll	*(To Brest)* Did you lose something father?
Fr Brest	Only my appetite.
Moll	Ha! You poor man, without an eardrum or an appetite. *(Exit Moll)*
Fr Brest	*(Squirming, to canon)* Did you hear that? Did you hear that canon?
Canon Pratt	Eat your supper, like a good man.
Fr Brest	You call this mess a supper.
Fr Loran	Easy Phil, easy.
Canon Pratt	*(Fed up)* What in blazes do you want? Tell us and we'll

	get it for you. Anything to put an end to this perpetual whining.
Fr Brest	All I want is a decent meal. I want nothing fancy.
Canon Pratt	The Lord save us, there are millions starving in India and South America …
Fr Loran	And Peru …
Canon Pratt	And Peru. Do you ever think of them?
Fr Brest	You think of them. I have enough of a problem trying to stay alive myself.
Canon Pratt	*(Clucks tongue)* Will you like a good man, will you pour out the tea Fr Loran? *(Fr Loran proceeds to pour tea)*
Fr Brest	*(Change of tactics)* Look we are three grown men and there's no reason why we should be at loggerheads. Don't you agree canon?
Canon Pratt	*(Eager to heal friction)* That's what I'm always saying. If we can't iron out our differences at our age we have failed in our calling. By God Phil, I'm with you all the way. Let us try to pull together rather than apart.
Fr Loran	Wisely put canon. As the hymn says – You'll never walk alone.
Canon Pratt	Yes thank you. That's the spirit. Back to the good old days again, eh. Huh? Huh?
Fr Brest	I hope so canon. I fervently hope so. But to reach any degree of happiness in any walk of life certain little sacrifices, certain acts of kindness and thoughtfulness are called for, especially if this little community of ours is to be restored to that happy state we once knew. Right?
Fr Loran	Right.
Canon Pratt	Right.
Fr Brest	What I want to know *father*, is who should make the first sacrifice? Who should set the example? *(Indicates canon)* Would you say it should come from the top or the bottom?
Fr Loran	Oh, the top … the top … where else?
Fr Brest	And who is the top? Who is the leader in this house?
Fr Loran	Moll Kettle.
Fr Brest	Don't be facetious. Our leader is our canon.
Fr Loran	Of course. *(Shouts towards kitchen)* Sorry Moll.

Fr Brest	I have already made my sacrifice. I run a regular bingo session. That, to me, is the greatest sacrifice of all.
Canon Pratt	That's not a sacrifice. That is an elementary parish duty, an evening chore.
Fr Brest	You're wrong. For me it is the great sacrifice *(Shouts)* because I hate the damned thing. I detest it. I loathe and despise it. I have frequent nightmares that are filled with numbers ... red twenty-eight, green twenty-two, yellow fourteen, black forty-six ...
Fr Loran	No. No. No, black forty-seven.
Fr Brest	Black forty-seven?
Fr Loran	Don't you get it ... *(Points at plate)* the hunger ... the starvation ...? The great famine.
Fr Brest	Bingo will eventually be the death of me. I have become resigned to it. You have heard of the Cisco Kid, the Sundance Kid, not forgetting Billy the Kid but here before you is the original ... one and only ... Bingo Kid.
Canon Pratt	Might I ask what you are driving at father?
Fr Brest	Certainly canon. I am going to ask you, in the interests of harmony, to make a little sacrifice.
Canon Pratt	I'll go a reasonable length to restore harmony. What is it you expect of me?
Fr Brest	From now on canon, I want you to swap plates with me. *(There is a silence as this sinks in. Canon slowly lowers napkin with which he has been wiping his mouth. Canon's eyes fall to his own plate, slowly and move to Brest's)* It's not much. I shall endeavour to do full justice to your plate and while you are doing full justice to mine you can devote a little thought to the starving millions who are causing so much concern. *(To Loran)* What do you think father?
Fr Loran	It seems fair. It's not as if you were asking the canon to forego his meals. He will have yours. *(Canon shattered)*
Fr Brest	Exactly. Nobody can say it's unreasonable. What do you say canon? Are you prepared to make this small sacrifice?
Canon Pratt	I see nothing small about it.
Fr Brest	You don't infer then that my plate is not an adequate

	swap for yours?
Canon Pratt	I didn't say that.
Fr Brest	Then you agree.
Canon Pratt	Of course I agree. I've always set the lead in this presbytery.
Fr Loran	Hear. Hear. *(Hand on his shoulder)* Canon, you have taken the first important step towards a lasting peace. Would that the great powers of the world had half your courage at their peace talks.
Canon Pratt	I do what I can.
Fr Loran	*(Carried away)* Let's shake hands on it. *(All shake)*
Canon Pratt	*(Standing, rubs hands)* Ah, this is great. I am very happy lads, very happy indeed. And now I'm going to ask the two of you to make a little sacrifice ….
Fr Loran	Anything canon, anything.
Canon Pratt	As you both know Moll is not getting younger. What she really needs is a little serving girl to do the beds and shine the windows.
Fr Brest	Yes of course.
Canon Pratt	She refuses, however, to allow a girl inside the door. The poor woman is genuinely overworked and God knows 'tis hardly fair to her if you know what I mean …
Fr Brest	What do you mean canon?
Canon Pratt	Suppose the two of you were to make your own beds and be responsible for the tidiness of your own rooms. She says that this would be a great help to her.
Fr Brest	Canon I am a priest not a parlour maid … I … I …
Fr Loran	Take it easy Phil. It's not so awful. Any fool can make a bed. It's reasonable enough.
Canon Pratt	Well Philip?
Fr Brest	All right. I won't spoil sport.
Canon Pratt	*(Sits)* There are good times coming. Thanks be to the good God, say I. *(Enter Moll)*
Moll	There's some apple pie and custard if anyone would care for some.
Fr Brest	Bring it on woman. Bring it on. *(Rubbing hands and going to table. Exit Moll. Sitting down, spoon in one hand, fork in*

	the other) Even as a child I had a particular longing for apple pie and custard. My mother used to specialise in apple pies. I must get her to send you one canon.
Canon Pratt	That would be nice.
Fr Brest	*(Extremely good cheer)* We had our own orchard, still have in fact. It's a wonder you never thought of planting a few fruit trees canon.
Canon Pratt	No time.
Fr Brest	There's a good market for fresh fruit.
	(Enter Moll, bearing a tray on which there are three dessert plates. She places one in front of each, the canon first, Fr Loran second, and Fr Brest third)
Moll	*(To canon)* One for the master. *(Places plate in front of him)* One for the dame. *(She places plate in front of him)* And one for the little boy that lives down the lane. *(She places largest plate in front of Fr Brest)*
Fr Brest	*(Rubs his hands)* This is fabulous. This is the loveliest and the largest dish of apple pie and custard I have ever seen. Thank you Moll.
Moll	Don't mention it father.
Fr Brest	*(Seizing spoon and adjusting himself on chair)* This is really something. *(The canon coughs politely in Fr Brest's direction)* Yes canon?
	(The canon points at Fr Brest's plate and then points at himself with a most polite smile. Fr Brest is puzzled. Canon hands his plate to Fr Brest. Brest accepts it, still wondering. Then it dawns on him. He lifts his own plate and reluctantly hands it to the canon who accepts it cheerily. Canon wires into it watched by Brest and Loran. Moll laughs and exits)

Canon Pratt	They happen all around us every day but mostly we don't even recognise them. I am talking about God's little miracles. *(Enter Bridgie, heavily pregnant)* There's a saying to cover it, what in blazes is it now…? Oh, yes, 'God works in mysterious ways'. You've often heard that said, no doubt. Well, 'tis none the less true for that.

Sure who'd have thought that Fr Loran, a man without the echo of a note in his head, would be after running a choir? God alone knows. And He must have given the hint to Moll Kettle for wasn't it she who organised it?

Oh, yes, there was a great deal of honest activity going on in Ballast during Moll's time at the presbytery. And thanks be to God, says I. |

Moll reads the paper by the fire. Fr Brest tries fixing his bingo machine.

Moll	*(Referring to the paper)* There's a picture in here of the new school. Wasn't it a lucky day the canon hired me four years ago! Look what I done. I built as fine a school as you'd see in Ireland and today 'tis being opened. 'Tis a great pity the bishop can't be here … but sure we can't have everything.
Fr Brest	You really think it was you and you alone who built the school?
Moll	'Twas me and the bingo.
Fr Brest	Bingo … the ultimate role of the Catholic Church in Ireland … the propagation of bingo.
Moll	May God forgive you.
Fr Brest	Where's the canon?
Moll	Bed.
Fr Brest	This hour of the day? Is he sick or what?
Moll	He's fine boybawn, thanks be to God. He's resting for the celebrations. I don't see your name here.
Fr Brest	Where?

Moll	The new list of diocesan appointments.
Fr Brest	How in the name of God would my name be there when old fogies of eighty and more won't give up the ghost? You'd think they would have the grace to retire and give the younger men a chance.
Moll	A chance at what?
Fr Brest	A chance to prove ourselves, to bring decaying parishes up-to-date, to get with it.
Moll	A lot you did with this decaying parish until I arrived and a lot you'd do now if you were let at it yourself. Where would you get the money?
Fr Brest	*(Bluffing)* God is good.
Moll	And bingo is good and raffles is good and jumble sales is good.
Fr Brest	*(Getting up)* Yirra, jumble rubbish … By the way, did you see my golf clubs anywhere?
Moll	Golf clubs? Yirra you have no time for golf boybawn, the man that has 'em now has his handicap down to nine.
Fr Brest	Haw?
Moll	And they raised three ten for the new school.
Fr Brest	Do you mean to stand there and tell me …?
Moll	Yirra blast you, what do I care about you?
Fr Brest	That's a nice way to address a priest.
Moll	If you don't learn how to master that contraption your balls will be all over the place tonight.
Fr Brest	Oh dear God but you're a terrible creature altogether but the Church will master you in the end.
Moll	And pray what have I to do with the Church? Sure an altar boy is higher up in the Church than I am.
Fr Brest	There's one great consolation.
Moll	What would that be?
Fr Brest	When the canon's day comes you're for the high jump. You'll go the road of Hitler and Stalin and all the other tyrants.
Moll	If I do I'll have something to show for my time.
Fr Brest	You don't have to tell me. By God you must have a right few quid made out of the Mass cards *(Looking back at her)*, not to mention the butcher and the baker and the

	grocer and any place else you could rob a halfpenny.
Moll	I have as much rights as you have and when you're going to the bishop let me know and I'll go with you. And if you're not satisfied with the bishop we'll go to the cardinal and if you're not satisfied with the cardinal we'll go to the pope.
Fr Brest	You're mad, stone mad.
Moll	Come on. You're the one that wanted to go to the bishop, aren't you? Always talking about it behind my back. Come on and we'll tell him that there's a new school since I came to this parish and we'll tell him the church is repaired and all the debts paid, all since I came.
Fr Brest	It was our work, mine and Fr Loran's.

(Enter Fr Loran, coatless and wearing dust turban. He carries a vacuum cleaner under his arm and a mop and pail in his hand)

Fr Loran	I've just done my room. Do you want me to do yours?
Fr Brest	No thank you.
Fr Loran	I'll give it a hoover so.
Fr Brest	I'm all right. I told you I can pull my weight.
Fr Loran	You mustn't fret yourself.
Fr Brest	I'm not fretting myself. *(Indicates Moll)* This monster here has me upset. She won't rest happy till she has me under the clay.
Fr Loran	Now, now, Phil, you mustn't let her get at you. I just ignore her.
Moll	Listen to the Mohammedan with the turban on his poll. A pity the bishop couldn't see you now.
Fr Loran	*(Mustering dignity)* Varium et mutabile semper femina.
Fr Brest	Well spoken Fr Loran.
Moll	*(In spite)* In nomina domina gomina, goose-grease galorum, sago lumbago tapioca semolina and if you don't like the music you can change the band, and if you're going to do any hoovering here boybawn forget it. I want to have a snooze before the festivities.

(Fr Loran hoovers; Fr Brest busies himself about his bingo machine and Moll after a few moments looking at the paper appears to doze off. As the hoovering stops Brest and Loran

are struck by the silence in the room and eventually focusing on Moll they realise she is asleep, the newspaper covering her face)

Fr Brest	Look at her. You'd swear butter wouldn't melt in her mouth. The devil incarnate.
Fr Loran	The devil?
Fr Brest	Who but a devil or an evil spirit would interfere with my sermon on mixed marriages? 'Mixed marriages how are you?' says she, ''twould be more in your line to give a sermon on mixed bread'.
Fr Loran	*(Now moving in closer to Moll)* Phil, maybe she is possessed.
Fr Brest	The devil has more sense.
Fr Loran	No seriously, she's dozing. This may be the only chance we ever have to exorcise her.

(Fr Brest is about to protest but Loran is gone like a shot to get the accoutrements for the exorcism. Brest remains sceptical but interested throughout the following. Loran re-enters wearing purple stole and carrying a lit candle and holy water font and sprinkler. Still wearing the apron and turban from his cleaning duties, he cuts a bizarre figure)

Fr Brest	I don't like this one bit. Maybe it might be better if we made contact with the official diocesan exorcist.
Fr Loran	He'd never agree and she'd never submit. We'd have to tie her down.
Fr Brest	Suppose something goes wrong!
Fr Loran	It's a chance we have to take. Look it's for her own good. There's no doubt but she's possessed. There's no other explanation for her diabolical behaviour. Here … hold this. *(He hands him holy water vat and sprinkler. Fr Loran finds book in his vestments and, wetting his thumb, locates appropriate page. He approaches Moll and removes the newspaper. She stirs uneasily but does not wake. Solemnly Fr Loran dips his sprinkler into the holy water vat. Moll opens her eyes while their backs are turned, looks up and falls quickly back to pretended sleep again)*
Fr Brest	The room first. *(Fr Loran dutifully sprinkles the entire room before addressing himself to Moll. He mutters some Latin while sprinkling. He gently sprinkles Moll. She stirs but does*

56

not waken) Easy for God's sake.

Fr Loran   O Lord we call on you now in our hour of great need, to rescue us from Satan and his minions. We ask you to free your poor servant Moll Kettle from the devil's tricks, that she might return to the path of goodness, gentleness, meekness. *(Moll opens her eyes and staring demoniacally at Brest and Loran chases them from the room. Collapses laughing in the chair as the canon enters)*

Canon Pratt   I brought you these empties, save you the trouble of getting them yourself.

Moll   There was no need to do that. Sit down by the fire and read your paper.

Canon Pratt   Anything good in it?

Moll   The pope says the world has gone to the dogs.

Canon Pratt   My mother used to say the same thing when I was a child.

Moll   People has no conscience these days.

Canon Pratt   Too well I know it.

Moll   Where's it going to end canon, with the women going around half naked? *(Canon clucks tongue reproachfully and nods his head in agreement)* They'll be wearing nothing at all soon.

Canon Pratt   The country is too cold for that.

Moll   When I was a girl, walking the streets with my friends, you would hear the hum of the holy Rosary from every home.

Canon Pratt   My God, yes.

Moll   And the beads rattling like horses' tackling. 'Tis the Beatles you'd hear now.

(The canon settles himself in his chair and reads his newspaper. There's a momentary lull)

Canon Pratt   Where were Frs Brest and Loran rushing off to Moll?

Moll   *(Twinkle in her eye)* The divil only knows canon.

Canon Pratt   They're very agitated these days Moll.

Moll   The Lord save us all canon, there's no meaning in the curates that's going these days. There's none of 'em want to do what they're told. Fr Brest is as bold as brass. God be with the fine curates we had when I was young. Pure saints they were with the eyes gone back

57

	in their heads and black rings under them like they'd be painted. Skin and bone and thin white faces, with the cheekbones standing out like corpses. 'Tis they were the holy men and 'twasn't their bellies was troubling them.
Canon Pratt	'Twas not indeed.
Moll	I remember one of Monsignor Mac Merrigan's first curates. You would swear he was after being whitewashed, the creature was so pale. He couldn't talk, only whisper. The Lord save us, but I tried every shop in the diocese to find a collar small enough for his neck. Sure he had no neck canon. 'Twas all Adam's apple. I often saw him stagger with the weakness on a cold morning …
Canon Pratt	Where's he now Moll?
Moll	He's in heaven canon. Where the hell else would he be!
Canon Pratt	Where else indeed, the poor man.
Moll	A canon now is different.
Canon Pratt	What should he be like now Moll? *(Preens himself)*
Moll	He should be fat and pleasant with a fine red face and a deep voice, like a bull, to frighten the sinners and to give the people confidence. Sure you would never see a thin canon. What would the people think if he wasn't round and shining and in prime condition.
Canon Pratt	Go on, go on.
Moll	A canon now should be a fine, rumbling, thundering man, well-fed and groomed so that his parish could boast of his appearance and be proud of him. He should have a fine thick neck, a severe face and a noble bearing to give him weight and holiness. Yourself now canon, is a fine example of what a canon should look like. Show me the priest, the monsignor used to say, and I'll tell you what the parish is like.
Canon Pratt	*(Preens himself)* I dare say there's a lot in what you say Moll. God knows you're not a woman that's given to exaggeration. I suppose there's no one would say that I'm not cut out for my job.
Moll	There's no one would deny it canon, no one. God save us but them curates of ours is a pure disgrace, that

	would eat you out of house and home instead of fasting and abstaining like the saints and martyrs.
Canon Pratt	Now, now, Moll, we mustn't be hard.
Moll	When I was handing up Brest his dinner the day you were away, he says to me, 'Where's the soup?' 'What soup is that boybawn?' I said to him. 'The soup before lunch,' says he. 'Soup is for invalids,' I told him. 'That's me,' says he. I tell you canon, when they start looking for soup before their dinner, they'll be looking for it after their dinner, sure isn't soup a dinner in itself canon?
Canon Pratt	A good plate of soup can be most nourishing.
	(Enter Fr Brest in an excited state)
Fr Brest	The bishop! The bishop!
Canon Pratt	What about the bishop?
Fr Brest	The bishop, he's coming.
Canon Pratt	Sure he can't be coming, sure isn't he way out foreign someplace.
Fr Brest	Well he's here now.
Canon Pratt	Oh Moll, there's nothing ready.
Moll	Calm down canon, calm down.
Fr Loran	His lordship, the bishop.
	(Enter a bishop in full regalia and humour. He is the master of the diocese)
Bishop	*(To Moll and canon)* Don't stand up. Don't stand up. You're looking well Connie. *(Expansively. As the canon kisses his ring)* None of that. No need for that.
Canon Pratt	A drink Moll. Get a drink for his lordship. A drink for everybody. Paddy Flaherty isn't it my lord?
Bishop	Yes. A drop of Paddy. Take a little wine Saint Paul says, for thy stomach's sake and for thy frequent infirmities. *(Exit Moll)* I was in Morocco. I woke up yesterday evening after lunch and looked out over the Mediterranean. This is very nice, very nice, I told myself, but isn't something happening in another part of the world? Isn't a school about to be opened, I said to myself. Isn't it about to be opened in my own diocese and isn't it to be opened by a substitute? Time I said to myself to be hitting for the green isle of Erin. Here I am ....

	(All applaud)
Fr Loran	Marvellous! Marvellous!
Fr Brest	To cut short his holiday.
Canon Pratt	It's what we expect of the man.
Fr Loran	Imagine from Morocco to Ballast!
Bishop	*(To canon)* It's a great credit to you Canon Pratt. Four years ago we had a ramshackle outhouse where you would be ashamed to send a decent scholar. *(To window. Looks out)* Now we have a school second to none. I am not unmindful of builders, those who further the cause of education are always in my mind, if you know what I mean. *(Enter Moll, bearing a tray on which are glasses. Puts tray and glasses on right of table near bishop. Whiskey on tray. Brest pours out drinks, gives one to bishop. Moll takes glass off table and gives it to canon)*
Moll	*(Distributing drinks)* Now would anyone like a drop of soup to keep them going till the festivities begin?
Bishop	Pray who have we here?
Canon Pratt	This is our housekeeper my lord.
	(Brest brings Loran down to left and is obviously arguing with him. 'Now is the time', Loran demurs)
Bishop	So this is Moll. *(Puts out hand, Moll kisses ring)*
Canon Pratt	You know of her?
Bishop	*(Retaining Moll's hand)* We know more than we are supposed to know Canon Pratt. *(Slaps her hand)* I have heard great accounts of Moll. *(Pats her shoulder, ushering her off)* Moll, fetch a drink for yourself and then we will all toast the great centre of education which is about to be declared open.
Moll	Yes, my Lord. *(Exit Moll)*
Bishop	*(To curates)* And now gentlemen, what's the score with the pair of you?
	(Suddenly faces them. Brest rather quickly and suddenly turns)
Fr Brest	We're fine, fine, my Lord.
Bishop	No grievances?
Fr Loran	No … no … not at all.
Bishop	A presbytery without grievances is paradise. Paradise does not come until we visit the next world. Speak up

	gentlemen.
Fr Loran	*(Prompted by Fr Brest)* Well, there's never a rose without a thorn your lordship.
Canon Pratt	*(Interjects)* They're always hopping balls my lord! Look at them. Did you ever see such health?
Fr Brest	Go on Joe. *(Loran hesitates. Brest fumes and is about to explode)* As the senior curate in this parish I …
Moll	*(Entering)* Here I am canon.
Canon Pratt	Will you be toastmaster my lord? Joe, will you like a good man get the parish camera, we'll record this for posterity. You don't mind my lord?
Bishop	Certainly not. Moll! *(Bishop beckons Moll over for photo)*
Moll	Me!
Bishop	Ladies and gentlemen, I bid you toast our new school. Long may it stand and may the scholars pour forth from its portals until Gabriel sounds his horn. Go maire sé go deo is go dtiocfaidh na scoláirí ó na hallaí ina sluaite. *(All quaff. Exit Moll)*
Fr Brest	My lord you asked earlier if we had any grievances. Well on our behalf Fr Loran would like to say a few words about conditions in this presbytery. Fr Loran?
	(Again Loran hesitates)
Bishop	*(To Loran)* Well what have you to say?
Fr Loran	What do you want me to say my lord?
Bishop	Say what's in your mind. Be frank. Be candid.
Fr Loran	Be candid about what my lord?
Bishop	About conditions in this presbytery.
Fr Loran	*(Unctuous)* I have no complaints my lord. I am only a curate.
Fr Brest	Only a curate … Tell him the truth ….
Fr Loran	*(All innocence)* The truth is my lord, that I personally have no complaints to make.
Fr Brest	Judas. Judas Iscariot.
Bishop	In a few moments I will be opening a new school, and after that I must go to suppress a Women's Lib movement in Lyracrompane. But I cannot leave unless there is peace in this house.

In Morocco I had time to think. *(To canon, turns to canon)* Canon Pratt you have served this diocese well. |

You have lived in obscurity in this out-of-the-way place for far too long. You have brought this parish out of the doldrums. You have given it a new school, a new status. You are the kind of canon who deserves better. *(Moves to canon, hand on shoulder)* For this reason I am appointing you to the parish of St Andrew in the city. You'll be happy there. I am sure that in no time at all you will be made a monsignor. It will be nice to have you near me in the city. *(Moves casually back to table)* Your age and experience will be assets to the diocese.

(Enter Moll. Bearing canon's comb, collar, surplice, and hat)

Canon Pratt   I don't know what to say … a monsignor … St Andrew's … Am I hearing things? Moll, do you hear this? We are bound for the city ….

Bishop   *(Turns: definitely)* You didn't hear me right father. You are bound for the city. Moll is not bound anywhere.

Canon Pratt   But …

Bishop   *(Hand raised)* Let there be no buts. The parish of Saint Andrew is run by an order of nuns.

Canon Pratt   But we've been together for so long.

Bishop   *(Facing canon)* The Church is a hard master canon, but hard as it is it isn't half as hard as a community of nuns. I would face the fires of hell on top of a bucking bronco before I would face a rampaging reverend mother. Moll stays here. Her assistance will be vital. The new parish priest will have a tough task before him.

Canon Pratt   Have you somebody in mind?

Bishop   Indeed I have. *(Turns: he looks at Fr Brest)* You may say I have. *(Fr Brest opens his mouth in astonishment and foolishly points a finger towards himself)*

Fr Brest   *(Disbelief)* Me?

Bishop   Who else father? *(Fr Brest staggers with the shock of it. He is supported by Fr Loran)*

Bishop   Fr Loran you will now be the senior curate. I will appoint a junior curate in due course.

Fr Loran   Is there any hope of a transfer my lord? *(Bishop laughs)* Oh God! If I knew the day I was ordained what was before me I'd have jacked the whole thing up and become a christian brother. Anything is better than being a curate.

Fr Brest	There are worse things in life father.
Fr Loran	*(Faces Fr Brest)* Name them.
Fr Brest	We'll have good times now Joe. Not to worry.
Bishop	Well canon. Shall we be on our way? There's a school to be opened and I'd like to see it first. *(Fr Loran opens door. They pass down stage of Fr Brest who moves up, if necessary, to make room for them. Bishop goes to door. Canon follows fairly slowly. Fr Brest a little to right, where canon blesses him)*
Canon Pratt	Of course my Lord. *(They are about to exit)* Oh, and, Moll – see the new parish priest about that 'little arrangement'. *(Exit canon)*
Fr Brest	What 'little arrangement'?
Moll	I'll talk to you later father.
Bishop	I'm sure you will. Has anyone any more to say? Come on. Now's the time. 'Tis no good talking about a bishop behind his back. All right then. May God's blessing be always on your ministry here Fr Brest. Be patient with your curates, thankful to your housekeeper and remember that incredible though it may seem now, I was once a curate too. God bless ye. *(Exit bishop)*
Fr Loran	You came out of it nicely.
Fr Brest	I was the senior curate.
Fr Loran	And I the junior.
Fr Brest	So long as you remember that we'll get on fine.
Fr Loran	I never thought I'd see the day.
Moll	'Twill be the best part of an hour before the school is opened. Will you take a drop of soup? I have it ready.
Fr Brest	All right all right. Let's have some soup. *(Exit Moll)* This will be a model parish. The new community centre will be an example to the rest of the country.
Fr Loran	Where will you get the money?
Fr Brest	I'll get it from the greatest source of all – from bingo. From now on we'll have bingo every night but it will be a bigger and a better bingo. *(Enter Moll with tray and two bowls of soup. One small, one large)* You hear me Moll, a bigger and better bingo.
Moll	I declare to God but you'll make a great parish priest entirely.

Fr Loran	How come we have different amounts?
Moll	What are you talking about?
Fr Loran	He has twice as much soup as I have.
Moll	If you don't like it, leave it.
Fr Loran	You saw the amount I got.
Fr Brest	In the name of God man I can't be bothered with these trifles. I have a big parish to run. You want to watch yourself, fall into line fast. I have only so much patience. Up to your organ loft and get the hang of this yoke between hymns. Bingo is now part of your job. Off you go now. *(Hands him the bingo machine)*
Fr Loran	A curate's lot is a hard one … *(Opens door)* there's no doubt but the curates of this country should be canonised. Canonised. *(Exits as bingo balls erupt from the machine)*
Fr Brest	It's not going to be easy Moll. That new community centre will cost money.
Moll	Put your legs up there and rest yourself. We have our bingo and what's to stop us having silver circles and raffles? If the money is there we'll get it out of them. You look out for me father and I'll look out for you and let the curates of this world look after themselves.

CURTAIN

THE CHASTITUTE

The scene is set as John Bosco tells his story from his own kitchen table. The table may remain throughout; we remain aware that he is recounting his story and illustrating it with scenes from his past.

All locations are suggested rather than realistic.

ACT ONE

ACT TWO

TO CECIL SHEEHAN

ACT ONE

SCENE ONE

Action takes place in the large kitchen of an old farmhouse in the south-west of Ireland. Night-time. Seated by a venerable Stanley Range is John Bosco McLaine. He is fiftyish, balding and decaying, sportily if badly dressed in bright tweeds. At the time he is polishing a shotgun. He drinks occasionally from a punch glass. He refills the glass from a large jug on the range. He puts the gun aside and rises. He takes glass with him and faces audience.

John   Look at me and tell me what you see. Go on. If you said I was a farmer you would be correct. That is what I am, a farmer, a bachelor farmer. It's the bachelor bit that complicates the whole business. I'll tell you the truth. What I am is a disaster. *(Swallows from glass)* This is punch I'm drinking. It's about the only thing I'm good at, the making of punch. Of course I shouldn't be drinking it. My doctor has warned me that if I don't give it up I'll soon be growing daisies. He says the liver is going. But what am I going to do if I stop drinking? *(Swallows again)* Maybe if I had married I'd be all right now. I tried. God knows I tried. I'd still marry any decent woman between thirty and the old age pension. But it's too late for that now. I muffed all my chances. *(Drinks)* You want to know why I am a disaster? You do? You don't? I'll tell you any way. In the first place my name is against me and it shouldn't be. John Bosco McLaine. It suggests a spoiled priest. It was my mother who insisted on the name. It was her contribution to the John Bosco canonisation movement. Twelve years after I was born John Giovanni Melchior Bosco was canonised a saint. My mother died happy, her choice of name was vindicated.

Voice   John Bosco, John ...

John   That'll be the aunt calling. *(Answers)* Yes auntie.

Voice   Is there somebody with you?

John   *(Calls back)* Nobody – more's the pity. *(To audience)* We had a heart to heart lately, the aunt and myself. I was sitting over there oiling my gun. *(Resumes seat by range)* I must have been talking to myself. She walked in out of the blue expecting to see somebody with me. *(Enter Aunt Jane)*

Jane:	*(Surprised at seeing nobody else)* Isn't there somebody else with you? You've been talking to yourself again. It's that punch. That stuff is going to kill you, you know that, John, don't you?
John	Nonsense.
Jane	You drink far too much John.
John	Just a few glasses.
Jane	At the rate you're going you're headed for disaster. *(Ponders a moment or two)* You know John I've been meaning to talk to you for some time. Please put that gun away and sit over here to the table. *(John does as she bids but brings punch jug and glass to table)* I'll come to the point John. I wasn't going to break it to you for some time but it's better this way. I'm getting married.
John	Married!
Jane	Yes married. He's a widower, older than I. We like each other God knows he's asked me often enough. Finally I said yes.
John	Congratulations Aunt Jane. I'm delighted for you, I really am. Do I get to give you away?
Jane	If you keep drinking the way you are I'll have to look for somebody else.
John	I'll cut it down I promise.
Jane	What worries me is that I may not be able to come for long weekends like I used to. You'll be alone here all of the time.
John	I'll be all right.
Jane	Not the way you're going! I have every notion of advertising for a housekeeper.
John	For me?
Jane	Who else?
John	You won't get any self-respecting woman to housekeep in this place. It's too isolated.
Jane	Not for the right person. What you need is a sound sensible woman, a widow maybe, someone who knows how to look after a man. Then ... after a while ... you never know how these things might turn out. It wouldn't be the first time a man married his housekeeper. But getting you a housekeeper is only one item on the agenda.
John	You mean you have other plans for me?
Jane	Frank, he's the man I plan to marry, well Frank is a man who doesn't let the grass grow under his feet. We put our heads together one night last week and you won't believe what we

	came up with.
John	Try me.
Jane	A matchmaker.
John	A matchmaker?
Jane	Yes.
John	I don't know any matchmaker ... Wait a minute you're not thinking of Mickey Molly?
Jane	Why not? He's married worse-looking than you and older than you and poorer than you.
John	But a matchmaker and Mickey Molly to boot!
Jane	Beggars can't be choosers John. The least you can do is meet the man and talk to him. You're not obliged to sample his wares. I've asked him to come over here tonight.
John	Tonight? But ...
Jane	That's settled then. *(Rises)* Now there's another thing.
John	What's that?
Jane	I've watched you a few times in the pub or at the hotel in Bannabeen. You just sit there ... drinking.
John	What do you expect me to do?
Jane	The place is literally crawling with women. Have you tried approaching one and offering her a drink? Think about it. I'll go and prepare that ad. *(Exit Aunt)*
John	*(To audience)* She doesn't know what's she's talking about. The unattached women of today burn up vodka and gin as if they had jet engines inside. If it made them drunk itself, but what happens is that they become more crafty with every dollop. I've been led up the garden path a hundred times. I softened them up but it was others who reaped the harvest. It was my groundwork made them lower their defences but it was always another who slipped in for the ko. That's the story of my life ... Nearly. I nearly got there a thousand times but nearly never bulled a cow. I've come close. Had a few narrow wides, even struck the crossbar but I never got the ball in the net. It's driving me crazy. Hard to believe, isn't it, in this day and age with morals at their lowest ebb, that I have yet to know a woman. *(Pours from jug into glass)* You know the two things that militated against my endeavours with the opposite sex? I'll tell you. Number one ... missionaries and number two ... townies. For townies you can read city slickers or any other

kind of pervert from a built up area. *(Swallows)* In my heyday the missionaries frightened the wits out of all the likely girls and women, even widows. I remember when I had the Baby Ford I had this young thing set up for the caper. A man with his own transport was half way towards seducing a girl in those halcyon days. Earlier that night she had attended the mission as indeed I had. There were two missionaries. This was a great gimmick entirely. You'd have the cross fellow and the quiet fellow moryah. The quiet fellow was all coaxing and cajolery never raising his voice. *(Two brown robed missionaries appear)*

Gentle M   Dearly beloved brethren. When evil thoughts assail you in the dark of the night, in the loneliness of your bed, pray, pray, for holy purity and dismiss those lascivious desires that are sent by Satan. Pray for holy purity and dwell not on thoughts of lust ... *(Muttering a prayer he withdraws)*

John   Now we come to the cross fellow. He would rant and rave and spray the first ten pews with showers of spittle.

Cross M   You have all of you lighted a match. You have all been burned by the flame and drawn back your hand and clutched it under your arm with the pain. Imagine a pain one million times worse, a pain that sears and blisters the entire body, a pain that cannot be endured so awful is its everlasting agony. *(Raises voice slowly until he is roaring at the top of his voice)* Can you imagine this indescribable torment? Well this is what awaits every fornicator and degenerate masturbator in this church ... *(He trembles, overcome. Exit)*

(Hymn – Faith of our Fathers)

John   See what I mean. *(Swallows)* There we were this girl and I , sitting happily in the Baby Ford. *(We see couple in Baby Ford, their actions suiting his words)* Earlier in the fish and chip shop after the pubs shut we had sated ourselves with chips and sausages. Only one hunger remained to be filled. The Baby Ford was parked overlooking a valley a few miles from town. Picture a fine full moon and a sky studded with twinkling stars. I was thirty years of age at the time with no conquest to show for it. A better setting for seduction you couldn't ask for. *(Swallows)* I'll never forget that night. I took her hand and squeezed it gently. She responded with a squeeze of her own and my heart pounded. I leaned over and kissed her. Ah she was a sweet innocent girl. Julia. That was her name, Julia. *(Swallows)* I shall never know what evil force prompted my next move. I daresay I thought it was the done thing. Without advance notice whatsoever I suddenly thrust my hand right up under her dress. She let out an unmerciful shriek but I held on. It was do or die.

Julia	Let go.
John	Never, never.
Julia	Let go or I'll report you to the missionaries. *(She runs from the car)* You ram, you dirty old ram. The vet should be got to you.
John	From under her dress something had come away in my hand. I looked at it. I couldn't believe my eyes. 'Twas a rosary beads. I know. I know. I know what you're going to say. You're going to ask what was a pair of rosary beads doing in a place like that. Sure, for God's sake, it was common practice at the time. The mothers used to stitch them to the gussets of the knickers so the daughters wouldn't surrender. The missionaries that put them up to it. *(The missionaries laugh – fade away. Enter Aunt Jane)*
Jane	What do you think of this now John dear? *(She reads from a slip of paper)* Housekeeper wanted. Sensible woman over thirty.
John	Sensible?
Jane	It's the word that's used. We don't want any doxies.
John	Don't we?
Jane	Of course not. *(Reads)* Widow would suit. To cater for gentleman of ...
John	*(Swallows, shrugs)* Fifty.
Jane	In early fifties! All right?
John	Fine.
Jane	Farmer. Transport to and from church. Good plain cook. Apply box number ...
John	Sounds all right.
Jane	It's not quite right. You wish to add anything?
John	No.
Jane	Have I omitted anything?
John	Don't think so.
Jane	By the way John what ever happened to that nice girl I introduced you to at the nurses dance a few years ago? What was

	her name?
John	Dora, Dora McMoo.
Jane	Fine girl. You seemed to hit it off with her as I recall.
John	Yes. For a while yes. It just petered out.
Jane	I'll type this. I'll go over it again. I'll let you see the end result before I send it. *(To herself)* Interesting person, Dora McMoo, probably married by now. *(Exit Jane)*
John	Dora McMoo. Another muffed chance. I remember the first time I met her. It was the aunt who introduced us. I resolved to bide my time on this one. I didn't want her erupting from the back of the car like Julia. It was a lovely summer's night. *(Couple in car suit action to John's narrative)* I was seated in the car with Dora. A fine buxom girl, no shortage of anything. We were parked in a shady spot, overlooking the river, only this time it was Cork City. The light from the street lamps was reflected in the water. I remember well three swans emerged out of the upriver reaches like fairy barques. Beside me Dora sat still, breathing evenly and serenely. My heart thumped and pumped inside me till I thought 'twould burst. The minutes passed. One, then two, then five, six, seven, eight, nine, ten. I didn't want to muff my chances. I was ever mindful of Julia and the rosary beads. I bided my time. I heard her sigh beside me. After a while she sighed again and again. Then came a long lingering sigh more like a ullagone.
Dora	Sweet John Joseph Alaphonsus Jesus are you dead or alive?
John	With that she banged the car door in my face. I heard afterwards on good authority that she was the hottest commodity between here and San Francisco. I had muffed it again. This time I was too slow. That's the story of my life. Too slow when I should be fast, too fast when I should be slow. *(Takes a goodly swallow and replenishes glass from jug. Enter Aunt Jane)* What now?
Jane	Will I put it in all the papers or just the local?
John	Suit yourself. I still don't think it will do any good. They all want the bright lights.
Jane	Not all John. There are some who like it quiet and peaceful. I know.
John	Very well put it in all the papers. In for a penny in for a pound.
Jane	That's the spirit. One final, all-out assault for better or worse.

	Just check me out on this John. Required urgently house-keeper. Thirty to fifty.
John	Make that sixty.
Jane	Very well. *(She pencils in new age)* Required urgently. House-keeper aged thirty to sixty. To cater for single farmer, early fifties.
John	Make that late forties.
Jane	Very well. *(She makes necessary adjustment)* Late forties. Excellent wages and conditions. Transport to and from church. References essential. Apply box whatever the number is ... What do you think?
John	No harm in trying.
Jane	*(Folds slip)* Please God now we'll have results. *(There is a knock on the door, off)* I'll see who that is. *(Exit Aunt Jane)*
John	I had ads in the papers before you know. Oh not for a house-keeper, nothing so prosaic. I advertised for the real thing. 'Respectable farmer, early forties. Owns up to date dwelling house, H & C. and car. R. C. Wishes to meet nice girl, twenty-five to thirty-five with a view to above.' In the beginning I had results of a kind. Unfortunately they were twice the age they pretended to be. The younger girls, of course, ignore such notices. I tried again lately. 'Lonely farmer, early fifties, wishes to meet partner, middle-aged with a view to matrimony.' I left it go too late. I know now with hindsight that a woman is never too old. When you're as desperate as I am there is no such thing as an old woman. *(Enter Aunt Jane followed by Mickey Molly. A week's beard adorns Mickey's face. He wears an old felt hat and a long black overcoat)*
Jane	You know Mickey Molly, don't you John?
John	Everybody knows Mickey Molly. How are you Mickey?
Mickey	Very well Mr McLaine thank you. Nice enough weather we're having these days.
John	Not bad at all.
Mickey	Bit of frost at night but of course that's a great sign. Frost is the boy to settle the weather. Frost, of course, is all very fine for them that's not out in it.
John	Shove up to the fire Mickey. *(Mickey moves up)* Will you have a bite to eat?
Mickey	I'm only after the supper Mr McLaine. Thanks all the same.

Jane	What about a nice cup of tea?
Mickey	No tea for me. I'd rather chance a drop of what yourself is taking Mr McLaine.
John	Of course, of course. *(Goes to range for jug)*
Jane	I'll fetch a glass.
John	Sit down Mickey. *(He pours into glass which Aunt Jane has placed on the table)*
Mickey	*(Raising glass)* Here's good health to you Mr McLaine and to you too Miss. *(Sits down)* I'm a busy man Mr McLaine so let's get down to cases. *(Aunt Jane sits as does John Bosco)*
Jane	As you have no doubt already guessed, Mr Molly, John here wants a woman.
Mickey	Is it a woman to marry?
Jane	Yes indeed, a woman to marry.
Mickey	He left it go a bit late didn't he?
Jane	You mean you can't help?
Mickey	I didn't say that Miss McLaine. What I mean is that he has the mileage up and when the mileage is up the field is cut down. It's a hard thing to have to say but facts is facts and figures is figures.
Jane	But you can help?
Mickey	Maybe. It all depends on what he wants.
John	All I ever wanted was a decent type of girl.
Jane	He doesn't want one of these modern misses, one of these so-called libbers. You know the type I mean.
Mickey	I don't deal in that sort of dame Miss McLaine. The likes o' them cocks up their noses at the likes o' me. These modern damsels don't know rightly where they're heading. 'Tis nothing these days but booze, sex and discos.
Jane	True for you. Too true.
Mickey	I'll tell you one thing and one thing alone about the doxies of the present time Miss McLaine.
Jane	What would that be?
Mickey	They all wants the bull but none of 'em wants the calf.
Jane	Well now we know what John here wants. Just a plain decent woman if that's not asking for too much.
Mickey	Indeed it's not. I have a few good class mares that might suit. What you want Mr McLaine is a good, steady, well-bred sort of mare that won't shy nor kick off the traces and that won't

	turn into a runaway.
John	I wish you would not refer to women as though they were beasts of burden. I simply want a wife if it's not too late in the day.
Mickey	I know. I know. I know what you want. There is first of all, however, a few questions to be asked. You may not like their tone but 'tis me that will have to face the firing squad if things don't work out in the marriage bed. When the works collapse the engineer must answer. Now Mr McLaine my lovely decent man answer truthful and all will be well.
John	Ask your questions.
Mickey	I will. I will. *(Pauses)*
John	Go on.
Mickey	I can't. *(Glances at Aunt Jane)*
John	Why can't you?
Mickey	A lady's ears might crinkle.
Jane	I get the message.
Mickey	Only for a few minutes Miss McLaine.
Jane	That's quite all right Mr Molly. *(Exit Aunt Jane)*
Mickey	Your exact fancy so as I can go as near as I can to meeting your wants.
John	I ... I don't know. I'm not sure.
Mickey	Very well. Do you want lean or thin, do you want rangy or butty ... Would you go for grandeur or would you like them that's down to earth? Would you go for a holy Josie or a one that's forgotten the altar? Take your time now. We have the night long.
John	It's ... It's the girl herself that would matter. Her ... her disposition. You know what I mean. Her way, her manner.
Mickey	My lovely innocent man there is no comparing a girl's manner before marriage with her manner after marriage, as many an unfortunate man knows to his cost, but have it your way. 'Tis you'll be living with her not me. That's the purpose of these questions, to find out exactly what you want and to divide that by what we can get for you.
John	What I'd like is a gentle sincere woman who's not gone from it, someone I can get along with and be seen with.
Mickey	I think I'm beginning to understand Mr McLaine. I'm getting to have a fairly clear picture of your requirements. *(Swallows*

as does John. John replenishes both glasses) Now Mr McLaine we'll start with the personal stuff.

John	Personal stuff?
Mickey	Your personal accoutrements.
John	My what?
Mickey	Just answer my questions and all will be made known. Do you strip good?
John	I don't follow.
Mickey	What are you like in your pelt?
John	What is the purpose of such a question?
Mickey	In God's name we'll get nowhere if you're to be diverting me. I'd just as soon go about my business.
John	Sorry. What was the question again?
Mickey	What are you like in your pelt?
John	May I take that to mean what am I like in the nude?
Mickey	You may indeed.
John	I'm no Apollo but I'm no bag of bones either.
Mickey	Is your belly slack?
John	Slack enough.
Mickey	Is your legs bandy?
John	My legs are OK.
Mickey	Is your natural belongings intact?
John	Natural belongings?
Mickey	In God's name is your undercarraige in good repair?
John	Oh ... I see.
Mickey	Is it in good repair?
John	I suppose so. But why are you asking such questions? What sort of woman would want such information?
Mickey	It's not the woman, Mr McLaine, but the woman's handlers.
John	Handlers?
Mickey	Father and mother. In some cases uncle and aunt or whoever is the guardian. You see my friend some of these marrying bucks aren't all they seem to be. The father and mother will want to be sure that you're possessed of the equipment to fulfil your side of the bargain.
John	This is like a bull inspection.
Mickey	Oh no. No inspection. They'll take your word which is more than civil because there is some I know would want a doctor's cert or a photograph. You're a man of honour. Your word will

	do. Many's the innocent girl, Mr McLaine, got a suck-in and found herself straddled by a man with no battery in his flash lamp. Happens all the time. Men will boast you know and women foolish enough to believe will be disappointed and deceived.
John	I can get a doctor to vouch for me.
Mickey	Your own say-so will do Mr McLaine.
John	There's nothing wrong in regard to what you mention.
Mickey	Good, good. I'm glad that's settled. It's always the trickiest part of this business. Now, is the house clear for a woman to come in? *(Explains)* Your aunt won't be a lodger?
John	No. I'll be completely alone. My aunt is getting married. I will be engaging a housekeeper, however, but naturally I would dispense with her services if I were to bring in a wife.
Mickey	Good. Very good. You're well away I take it?
John	You could say I'm moderately well off.
Mickey	I'll leave it at that for now. Are you free tomorrow night?
John	Yes.
Mickey	Can you present yourself at the Crossroads Pub?
John	Yes.
Mickey	Alone and unaided.
John	Yes.
Mickey	At the hour of nine?
John	Yes.
Mickey	I will introduce you then to a lady by the name of Norrie Macey. I will sit and talk with the two of you until such time as the ice is thawed. I'll leave ye to yeer own devices then.
John	I'll be there. What's she like?
Mickey	It's not what I think she's like but what you think she's like that matters. I'll bring the mare to the parade ring, it's for you to put her through her paces.
John	Tell me at least if she's presentable. *(Norrie in spotlight)*
Mickey	She's a dainty bit. No one would deny that. She has a good make, she's firm and she's not excitable. *(Rises)* She has an even temper. She won't vex and she won't snap. She's a kind little mare by any reckoning. Tomorrow night. *(Moves towards exit)* Nine. *(Pauses)* Be there. *(Exit Mickey)*

(CURTAIN)

ACT ONE

SCENE TWO

The following night. Action takes place at the Crossroads Bar. On a makeshift platform there is a one-man band, drum and organ. There is a counter at opposite end where drink is served by a barman in shirtsleeves and a towel over his shoulder. The one-man band is nearing the end of a waltz as John Bosco enters.

One-man *(Stentorian)* Come along now. Come along now. Take your partners for a tango.

Link *(John ... in high hopes. Smartens up. Action into Crossroads Bar, meets Norrie, who is already established in view. Music playing. Brief scene. Norrie just drinks and watches the goings on, as in script. John flounders and tries to make conversation over loud music. Maybe he asks her to dance. She suddenly stands up without a word and walks out on him)*

Mickey *(Joining John as Norrie exits)* How did you get on?

John Fair.

Mickey Fair?

John All right, I suppose.

Mickey You don't sound very enthusiastic. What went wrong?

John I don't know. There was something weird about her.

Mickey Weird?

John She never spoke. Just drank and watched the goings-on around her,

Mickey There's many would hold with women not talking. Did you talk yourself?

John I may have passed a few remarks about the weather.

Mickey The weather has a lot to answer for. Put the weather from your mind the next time you meet her. Shove in nice and close to her and ask her does her toes be cold when she's in bed. Ask her if she sleeps heavy or light, left side or right side, on her back or her belly or maybe 'tis how she does be tossing and tumbling all night. Find out. Ply her with strong drink and nice comfortable questions of the cosy kind. Right?

John Right.

78

(The music starts. Enter Sylvester. During the following Sylvester picks up Juleen and they dance the tango to excess)

Mickey   There he is, the one and only Sylvester Brady. I know him by eyesight. A regular lady-dazzler as the song says. They say that all he has to do is top the cigarette, give a flick of the eyebrows and the belle of the ball is in his arms

John   The girl is one of the McCoons, isn't she?

Mickey   Juleen McCoon. Juleen McCoon from Tubbernaroon.

John   They all say she's a flier.

Mickey   Oh they do indeed, especially them that were never with her. As I recall however, she has been mentioned in dispatches for services, you might say, above and beyond the call of duty. Have you approached her?

John   Waste of time. Me and my equals have no chance against the likes of Brady. He's a liar and a cheat and he's landed innumerable girls in trouble – and he's a townie to boot – and still women go mad for him, at least the women around here.

Mickey   Could this be envy?

John   Envy? Him?

Mickey   Could your dislike of him be due to his success with Juleen McCoon and all the other Juleen McCoons of the countryside?

John   It's possible I suppose.

Mickey   Then you'd want to change your tack my friend. Beggars can't be choosers you know.

John   What's that supposed to mean?

Mickey   It means you can't afford to be hostile towards this Sylvester Brady. He holds all the aces. There's more to be gained by joining up with him than by crossing him.

John   Join up with that fellow. Never.

Mickey   Remember Brady's in. You're out. Dang it man, buy the hoor a drink can't you. Pretend you like him even if you don't. Watch his style. Find out what it is about him that so impresses the ladies. The man is a master of his trade. Serve your time to him and you can be master too. *(They watch Sylvester as he cavorts about. The dance ends)*

Mickey   Quick. Call him over.

John   I couldn't.

Mickey   For God's sake call him. You can't afford not to. Go on man.

John	*(Calls)* Eh, Mr Brady. *(John raises hand. Sylvester turns, points finger at chest to confirm that he's the one)*
Mickey	*(Calls)* Come on over here. *(Sylvester comes to table)* Ah Mr Brady how are you sir? Will you join us for a taoscawn?
Sylvester	All right. I'll have a drink with you.
Mickey	What'll it be?
Sylvester	Remy Martin. Large.
Mickey	A large Remy Martin! I see. What's yours John?
John	Small Irish.
Sylvester	Bring a ginger ale will you?
Mickey	Small Irish, large Remy Martin, ginger ale. *(Moves to bar counter)*
John	How's things?
Sylvester	Things?
John	You know ... happenings!
Sylvester	What sort of happenings?
John	General happenings.
Sylvester	You mean women don't you?
John	I suppose so.
Sylvester	Why the hell can't you say so?
John	All right. Womanwise how are things?
Sylvester	Can't complain. Wasn't that Norrie Macey I saw you with?
John	Y ... es.
Sylvester	Was it Mickey Molly fixed you up there?
John	He introduced us if that's what you mean.
Sylvester	That's not what I mean.
John	Then what do you mean?
Sylvester	Mickey Molly's been matchmaking for you with Norrie Macey.
John	What of it?
Sylvester	What of it he says? Very well. Stick to that attitude and you'll find out too late.
John	Sorry. I'd like to find out now.
Sylvester	About this Norrie Macey. You know she's called the seven day wonder
John	No.
Sylvester	How could you? Mickey Molly didn't tell you that. You want to know why she's called the seven-day wonder?
John	Please.
Sylvester	Because they say she has seven children, all farmed out now,

	of course. A child for every day of the week.
John	I didn't know she was married before.
Sylvester	She was married neither before nor after.
John	But the children?
Sylvester	All sired by visiting dignitaries, van salesmen, showband musicians, mobile kitchen operators, itinerant evangelists, take your pick.
John	I'd never have guessed.
Sylvester	A liberal soul, my friend, to say the least, God bless the creature. She'll marry you, of course, if that's what you want. There will be a clause, however.
John	A clause?
Sylvester	You ask her to marry you in the morning and she'll say yes .... yes, of course, I'll marry you but ... I'm not going to leave down my regular clients.
John	Good God!
Sylvester	You steer clear of Norrie Macey.
John	Thanks for the tip.
Sylvester	That's all right. If you ever want your card marked you know where to come.
John	What about the one you were dancing with?
Sylvester	Juleen is it?
John	Well?
Sylvester	No tales out of school pal. Just remember one thing Juleen McCoon carries my brand OK?
John	OK.
Sylvester	These country kittens go wild for me. I'm not boasting. I just happen to have what they want. There's no accounting for tastes.
John	Don't I know. I had a half-wit who used to work for me and now he's married to a beautiful Pakistani girl in Camden Town while I can't get a woman of any kind.
Sylvester	What say we do something about that?
John	You mean you'd help?
Sylvester	I said I'd mark your card didn't I? You want me to mark your card?
John	Of course. Of course.
	(Mickey arrives and deposits tray of drinks on table)
Mickey	What have you two been up to?

John	Sylvester promises to help me.
Mickey	Well I'll certainly drink to that. *(All quaff)* Any immediate plans Sylvester?
Sylvester	Rome wasn't built in a day Mickey.
Mickey	Rome was not Mr Brady.
Sylvester	*(To John)* You free on Sunday night next?
John	*(Nods eagerly)* Yes.
Mickey	For God's sake he's always free.
Sylvester	Can you drive me to Cork?
John	Anywhere.
Sylvester	You're on then. I'll be out at your place by six o' clock. You bring enough money and you'll have a night to remember. I'm a little short just now so make sure you bring enough for two.
Mickey	He'll do that, won't you, John.
John	Sure, Sure. That's no problem. I can collect you in Bannabeen if you like.
Sylvester	And have every bum in town advertising our business? Not likely.
Mickey	He'll be ready when you call. I'll see to that.
Sylvester	You know Knackers' Lane in Cork?
John	Just to glance at in passing. I've never sojourned there.
Sylvester	You know the Three Roosters public house down at the end?
John	I've noticed the sign I've never been in.
Sylvester	You've never been anywhere have you son?
Mickey	That's all about to change now though.
Sylvester	*(Lays a hand on John's shoulder)* You might say my lad that your life is only beginning. We'll lay that bogey of yours in the Three Roosters or I'm a Dutchman. *(To Mickey)* Why didn't you tell him about Norrie Macey's pedigree?
Mickey	Why should I?
Sylvester	He's your client.
Mickey	So is she.
	(Juleen McCoon appears at table)
Juleen	They're playing our song Sylvie.
Sylvester	I can hear. *(The one-man band is playing a tango)* Until Sunday my friend. You're with the right mentor now. My track record is impeccable. I go back a long time. I was seduced by a sixty-year-old deserted wife when I was fifteen. After that auspi-

cious beginning I've never looked back. *(Sylvester dances off with Juleen. John Bosco comes forward for narrating. He is joined by Sylvester, Heather and a gaudy bird. On cue Sylvester steers bird away)*

(Curtain)

Link/John *(Reminiscing to audience)* We left for Cork in the afternoon. You can only be a success, he said, if you refuse to be diverted. You must have a one-track mind, said he, if you are to flush the bird. I honestly felt my days as a chastitute were over. Chastitute! The word was coined by our parish priest Fr Kimmerley. According to him a chastitute is a person without holy orders who has never lain down with a woman. He or she, as the case may be, is a rustic celibate by force of circumstance, peculiar to countrysides where the Catholic tradition of life-long sexual abstemiousness is encouraged and defended by the Catholic Church under whose strictures free-range sex is absolutely taboo. I am, therefore, a chastitute. So much for that. In the Three Roosters Sylvester procured a pair of prime doxies. He went his way with his and I went my way with mine.

ACT ONE

SCENE THREE

Action take place in an upstairs room in a house in Cork city. Light goes up in a dingy room which contains a bed, a chair, a small table and a wardrobe. Enter a woman, thirtyish, heavily made-up, wearing a headscarf and raincoat. She carries her shoes in her hand. Upon entering she flops on the side of the bed and takes off headscarf. She is Heather.

Heather   For God's sake Johnny come on. Come on. Everything's fine. We have the place to ourselves. *(Enter a tip-toeing John Bosco carrying shoes in one hand, brown paper bag of drinks in the other. He looks cautiously about)* See. Nobody here, just ourselves. Put the drink on the table, love. I'll get some glasses. *(Unsteadily she rises. She climbs on chair to search the top of the wardrobe. She fumbles around)* Should be here some place. *(Locates glass and hands it to John who has meanwhile placed a large bottle of vodka and some mixers on table)* You bought a full bottle, a whole full bottle of vodka. Sylvie was right. You are a pet. *(She hands him a second glass. She wobbles. She falls into his arms. They land on the bed. She kisses him. A cracked, female voice is heard off.)*

Voice   Is that you Heather? *(Silence)* Heather do you hear? Is that you? *(John jumps from bed and would be gone but Heather restrains him by holding his hand)*

Heather   Don't panic Johnny for God's sake. It's only my mother.

John   Your mother!

Heather   Not to worry. She's well used to this. What I mean is she's well used to visitors.

Voice   Are you all right Heather?

Heather   *(Calls back)* Yes mother I'm all right. *(To John)* Best give me a few pounds. It'll keep her quiet. *(Calls)* I'll be right in mother.

John   Of course. *(He withdraws wallet, opens it and extends it.*

Heather   *(Leans forward to examine contents)* I'll just take two of these. That should do it. *(Rises)* Pour a drink love. I'll be right back. Don't go away now. *(Exit a staggering Heather. John pours drink into both glasses and listens apprehensively to female voices arguing off. Enter an unkempt man wearing pyjamas. He is Heather's brother. John is shocked, frightened)*

John	In God's name who are you? I mean no harm, I'm innocent. Nothing has happened.
Brother	I'm her brother.
John	Heather's brother?
Brother	Her brother, her only brother.
John	Oh. How do you do?
Brother	Are you the chap Sylvie was to bring?
John	Sylvie? You mean Sylvester. Yes I'm the man.
Brother	Have you any few cigarettes?
John	I don't smoke.
Brother	You wouldn't have the price of a package would you?
John	Of course. *(Willingly extracts his wallet and hands over a pound)*
Brother	Price of a drink?
John	Sure. *(Hands over another pound. Sounds of voices entering)*
Brother	Not a word about this.
John	Oh not a word. *(Brother hastily exits. Enter Heather with mother who wears night-cap and pyjamas)*
Heather	I'm sorry about this but she insisted on meeting you. Mother this is Johnny. I invited him home for a drink.
Mother	*(Grand Cork accent affected)* How do you do?
John	How do you do?
Mother	You're not a native of Cork are you Mr ...?
John	McLaine. John ... Johnny ... Johnny McLaine. No. I'm from Kerry.
Mother	Kerry. I love Kerry people. Heather's father, God rest him, used to go to Kerry a lot. He was a commercial traveller you know. Most respected.
Heather	Mother please. Not now. *(Swallows drinks in toto. Holds onto bed)*
Mother	He did all Kerry and Limerick.
John	What line was he in?
Mother	Sundries.
John	Sundries?
Mother	Zips, hooks and eyes, garter elastic, buttons, studs, moth balls, blotting paper, everything and anything. We had our own car in those days. There was not a weekend we didn't go somewhere. He was a most respected man, most respected. Connected with the bishop, through his mother's people. Oh a most respected man, a daily communicant. We had a ser-

85

vant girl then. She was from Kerry too. Maggie something or other. My own people, of course, were connected with all the best families. My husband was most respected, oh most respected. Then one morning he just went off like that! *(Clicks her fingers)* A stroke coming from the altar. Never recovered. Went straight to Heaven ... The wreaths, the mass cards, the telegrams. How many wreaths was there Heather?

Heather *(Who is pouring another drink)* I forget mother. Look why don't you go to bed?

Mother Very well if that's what you want. Goodnight Mr ... Johnny. Goodnight Johnny. You must come around for tea some evening Johnny. *(Exits muttering)*

John Goodnight missus ...

Heather You mustn't take any notice of her. *(She hands him his glass)* Let's have a toast ... to us. *(She clinks her glass against his. Lays her glass on the table and starts to take off her coat. John helps take off coat. He lays it gently across the bed)* Don't put it there. It won't be worth tuppence.

John Sorry.

Heather Put it in the wardrobe. I won't be needing it again. Do you go out with many girls?

John Not many. I haven't been out with a girl in *(Pauses)* ages. *(He opens wardrobe and hangs coat. Heather fumbles with dress)*

Heather Undo my back buttons will you Johnny? *(John does her bidding)* I can tell you're not used to this.

John To what?

Heather To unbuttoning dresses. *(She swallows the contents of her glass)*

John Another drink? *(He takes glass and half fills it. Uncorks mixer bottle and adds)*

Heather Are you married?

John No.

Heather I was engaged once. A doctor, a surgeon in the Regional. We had a date fixed, cake ordered, trousseau bought, guests invited, everything.

John What happened?.

Heather Died, car crash. He adored me. I could have had anybody, barristers, dentists, professors, anybody. He was the only one. I'll probably never marry now. I could be married tomorrow if I wanted. There's an army captain mad after me. He says he'll shoot himself if I don't announce the date. I've told him it's no good. *(She pulls her dress over her head. Speaks from beneath it)* I vowed I'd never do a steady line after my fiance died. He was the only one. Help me with this. Take the end and pull. *(John takes end of dress and pulls it over her head and off. Underneath she wears a slip)* You're the first one since he died. You really are.

John	Of course. *(She sits on the bed. Drains her glass)* You want another drink?
Heather	*(Very drunk now)* Sure. Arthur is his name.
John	Who?
Heather	The captain. Arthur, Arthur Dangleby. *(John adds from mixer)* He sends me flowers all the time. *(John hands her drink)* You're shy. Are you shy? Are you shy Johnny? *(John takes refuge in his glass)* Don't be shy Johnny. There's no need to be shy with me.
John	Where do you work?
Heather	By day you mean?
John	Well ... yes.
Heather	The bacon factory. I'm a supervisor. I don't work there anymore though. This foreman, a married man with six kids, wanted to get off with me. I'm not that kind of girl. I just couldn't stay on. Here, hold this. *(She hands him glass. She pulls slip over head and awkwardly manages to get it off. She throws it to one side. She sits on bed in bra and panties)* My hair must be a sight.
John	It's lovely.
Heather	You're just saying that.
John	No. No. I mean it. Honestly it's lovely.
Heather	Drink. *(John hands her the glass. She swallows last drop, allows glass to fall to the floor. Head droops and she closes her eyes barely balancing herself upright with hands resting on the bed. She sighs again and there is the faint rumble of a snore followed by a fitful snort or two. Then comes a full-bodied snore. She falls forward helplessly but he checks her. She resumes former position somewhat precariously. She snores again)*
John	Heather, Heather. *(Shakes her shoulder gently)*
Heather	*(Opening eyes for a moment)* What? What time is it? Where am I?
John	Remember me? Johnny?

Heather   *(Trying to focus her eyes on him)* Johnny! Johnny who? *(She snores deeply and relapses into sleep. She falls back helplessly onto bed and to profound slumber. John stands looking at her briefly and then locates his shoes)*

John   Goodnight ... Heather. *(There is no answer from the bed save a snore. Exit John, tip-toeing with shoes in hand)*

(CURTAIN)

Link   John wonders why did he allow Heather to get filled with booze and pass out uselessly. He took a few days to recover from the shock and get back from Cork. He found that in the meantime Aunt Jane had found Eva through an advertisement and installed her. *(The lights are coming up in the kitchen on Eva)* John full of dreams about the housekeeper, and what did he find ... *(We see the forbidding Eva)*

ACT ONE

SCENE FOUR

Action in kitchen. A severely dressed woman, all in black, stands ironing clothes at a kitchen table. She is the new housekeeper Eva Kishock. Enter John followed by Mickey Molly and Aunt Jane who is dressed for travel and carrying a large handbag. John put his shotgun carefully to one side.

Jane	I'm away Mrs Kishock. I like to be home before nightfall.
Eva	Very good Miss McLaine. When can we expect you again?
Jane	Not for some time I'm afraid. There are so many things to be seen to.
Eva	It won't be too long I hope.
Jane	Not too long. Are you quite happy here Mrs Kishock?
Eva	Quite content thank you Miss McLaine.
Jane	You don't miss the city?
Eva	Certainly not Miss McLaine.
Mickey	Was your late husband from the country or the city missus?
Eva	My late husband was a drunkard and that's all I'll say on the subject.
Mickey	Sorry to hear that missus.
Jane	I'm sure you and John Bosco will get along nicely. Well ... Goodbye then Mrs Kishock.
Eva	Goodbye Miss McLaine
John	I'll see you to the car.
Mickey	No, no, no need. I'll do that. You just stay where you are and make the most of your time. *(Mickey motion to John to make the most of his chances with Eva. Exit Mickey and Aunt Jane)*
John	*(Locates bottle and pours himself a drink)* Would you care for a drink?
Eva	No, thank you.
John	I'm glad you like it here ... You don't find it lonely?
Eva	No.
John	You don't miss the bustle of the city?
Eva	No.
John	You didn't have any family did you Eva?
Eva	If you don't mind Mr McLaine it will be Mrs Kishock not Eva.

John	Sorry.
Eva	Nothing to be sorry about, Mr McLaine, just as long as we know where we stand. You asked if I had a family?
John	It doesn't matter. It's none of my business anyway.
Eva	I had a daughter. She died when she was three..
John	Sorry.
Eva	There's nothing to be sorry about. It's all over and done with. All forgotten this long time. The last thing I want Mr McLaine is for a man to be sorry for me. *(She gathers bundle of shirts)*
John	I'll help with those.
Eva	You what?
John	Help you with ... the ... the clothes.
Eva	How can you help with these? There's hardly a pound weight in the lot. Knock it off Mr McLaine. *(She exits with clothes. Returns immediately to table where she returns iron to holder and folds pressing cloth)*
John	I'm afraid the social life around here leaves a lot to be desired.
Eva	I'm not here for the social life Mr McLaine.
John	I just meant if you felt like a drink there's a pub at the crossroads.
Eva	Mr McLaine there are a few things I'd like to make clear.
John	Fire away.
Eva	No offence intended but if the cap fits you know what you can do. I will not, under any circumstances whatsoever, be going for a drink with you. In fact I will not be going anywhere at any time with any man. I hope I make myself clear Mr McLaine.
John	Of course. I was just ...
Eva	I've been through this jig too many time Mr McLaine and I find it's important to get the message across early. There will be no familiarity, no confidential chit-chats, no outings, no lingering pats on the posterior ... *(John is about to protest)* Let me finish please. I'm not saying you are that kind of person Mr McLaine. I'm merely stating my position based upon past experiences. I am your housekeeper and nothing else. If I wanted the other kind of jazz I certainly wouldn't hang around here. I'm laying all of this on the table now in case we should happen to get our lines crossed in future. I want to make my position crystal clear.

John	Whatever you say Mrs Kishock. I was only trying to be sociable, make you feel at home.
Eva	Well it's not necessary I assure you. Just let me get on with my job Mr McLaine and you'll have no reason to complain. *(Gathers cloth and iron and exits. John swallows some of his drink and pours another. Enter Mickey)*
Mickey	Well?
John	Ice.
Mickey	Ice is there to be thawed.
John	There's no thawing this one.
Mickey	That's a pity. She's not a bad-looking piece.
John	There's a jinx on me. There has to be.
Mickey	No there isn't. You mustn't let that night in Cork get you down.
John	Cork was the biggest disaster of all. I'm a washout.
Mickey	Never. Never. *(Enter Eva with some linen which she places on the table. She is about to exit when Mickey forestalls her)* Whoa, whoa, whoa, whoa there! Whoa the blood.
Eva	Are you addressing me?
Mickey	Yourself it is. Stand aisy awhile and pass the time with us. God's sake we're not criminals.
Eva	What exactly do you want from me?
Mickey	Me is it? I wants nothing.
Eva	*(To John)* And you Mr McLaine?
John	Nothing, nothing at all. Just trying to be sociable.
Eva	Mr McLaine please don't put me in a position where I'll be forced to give you notice. I'll cook for you, sew for you, launder for you, keep your house trim but beyond that not an inch, because you see Mr McLaine I detest men for what they're after. I loathe and despise men. Every time I think of a man my stomach turns inside out. The only thing I feel like doing to a man is spitting on him. Excuse me now. *(Exit Eva)*
John	You can feel the cold draught after her. It's as though an iceberg had passed by. She must be the coldest creature God ever made and to think it fell to my lot to have her for a housekeeper.
Mickey	Icebergs melt, John, when the warm air circulates about them. Basically there's three kinds of women. Cold, warm and hot. Your warm woman is your best woman but there's not enough

	warm women to go around so we are left with the cold and the hot. The hot is all appetite and consumes too much too soon. Therefore, we must look to the cold.
John	Not this one. This one won't thaw.
Mickey	Don't be too sure. I know more about women than you ever dreamed of on a frosty night, and it's my guess there's a woman inside there somewhere and she's trying too hard to conceal it. I'll lay an acre of arable land to a square yard of cowdung that this damsel can be thawed.
John	Not by me. Mickey my friend at last I'm starting to see myself as others see me. The countryside is tainted by slowly withering blossoms like me. We can't be paired off or matched. We're in excess of the quota. People snigger at us. We're always good for a laugh. Look at me. Over fifty years of age without raising a flag. Over half a century without a kill.
Mickey	You're not being fair to yourself.
John	You know what really knocks the sap out of a man, the one thing that really makes him cringe?
Mickey	No.
John	It's when you're my age and a woman laughs at you because you're a man. That really makes a man feel ashamed. Dirty old men they call us because we dare aspire to having women of our own. *(Enter Eva)*
Eva	There is a gentleman at the back door Mr McLaine.
John	Did he give a name?
Eva	He says he is Monsignor Brady.
Mickey	That'll be the bould Sylvester.
John	Show him in please Mrs Kishock. *(Eva returns the way she came)*
Mickey	The right man in the right place.
John	I don't know all about that.
Mickey	He'll get you out of yourself. Invite him to the spring show. A talent like his deserves an airing in our capital city. You never know what he'll land you into, and that's what counts. Anything is better than wilting away here in the hills. *(Enter Sylvester and Eva. Men exchange glances)*
Eva	Will there be anything else Mr McLaine?
John	You're not retiring already?
Eva	Any objection?
John	No. No. Of course not.

Sylvester	Who is this ravishing creature?
John	Sorry. This is Eva Kishock my new housekeeper. Eva ... Mrs Kishock this is Sylvester Brady. *(They shake hands)*
Sylvester	Housekeeper eh? Some people have all the luck. How about a sandwich?
John	She's just retiring Sylvie.
Eva	It's all right Mr McLaine. What kind of sandwich do you require?
Sylvester	What kind of sandwich have you got?
Eva	Mutton, ham, cheese, tomato ...
Sylvester	A very good selection Eva. It will have to be Eva between us, all right? Make a ham sandwich with lashings of mustard. *(Eva goes about her business. Calls)* Don't be long will you Eva? I'm starving. *(Aside)* Eva, Eva I'll soon deceive ya. *(To John)* She's a sexy bit our Eva.
John	You'd need a blow lamp to thaw her out.
Sylvester	No blow-lamp needed there. That's just a facade, a defence mechanism. The right man with the right approach, at the right time is more than a match for the likes of your housekeeper. Are you interested?
John	She made it quite clear that she's not interested in me.
Sylvester	That doesn't answer my question.
John	Of course I'm interested.
Mickey	Dang it man he's interested in anything that's female.
Sylvester	All right then. Bide your time and I'll soften her crust.
John	Soften her crust indeed. With what?
Sylvester	With the common grease of guile my friend. *(Enter Eva)*
Eva	Your sandwich Mr Brady.
Sylvester	*(Accepts)* Sylvie's the name. Remember that. Sylvie. And you're Eva. Join us in a cup of tea Eva. The night is young.
Eva	I'm sure you will excuse me, Mr Brady. *(To John)* Breakfast will be on the table at half-past eight. *(Exit Eva)*
John	See ... she's frozen solid boy. You'll never come around a dame like that.
Sylvester	And I tell you Johnny boy that beneath that cold exterior churns the red lava of passion. She's a walking volcano. Just you be there when the gusher comes in and I promise you a crucible of lechery such as no man ever tasted. I tell you that even your bones will melt.

Mickey	Why don't you make a jug of punch John and we'll review our strategy.
Sylvester	And what array of blemished beauties have you lined up for him this time?
Mickey	I have been going back over my lists these nights and 'tis only a matter of time till I turn up the right trump. *(He produces jotter and proceeds to thumb through it)* If you like I'll name a few likely mares for your approval. *(Reads painfully)* Speckles Nora, Toordrumagowna, farmer's daughter, forty, so called because the belly is speckled with freckles as was seen when she wore a bikini to her father's meadow some short years ago.
Sylvester	Can't place her at once but go on.
Mickey	There's a Marian Year grotto next to the house.
Sylvester	Keep talking.
Mickey	A stand of spruce at the left if you take the Bannabeen road.
Sylvester	Colour hair?
Mickey	Black one day, brown the next. *(Sylvester shakes head)* She was at the farmers' social in the Bannabeen Arms last December.
Sylvester	So was I.
Mickey	Cast your mind back then to that occasion and ask yourself if you recall a lady as was wearing a green frock that left her bare along the entire broad of her back.
Sylvester	I have her. A good soul in her time. Widely known for her good nature. Reformed now I daresay and anxious to settle. Too long on the road. Too long in the tooth.
Mickey	She's not young but neither is she old.
Sylvester	Sixty if she's a day. This man is deserving of better.
Mickey	And what are we looking for? Isn't it only someone to make our beds and wet our tay and keep us company for the rest of our days with maybe a leg thrown over now and again. There's no Miss World or no Rose of Tralee goin' to make her way up here Sylvie.
Sylvester	Point taken.
Mickey	Lispie Suzie?
Sylvester	Pass on.
Mickey	What's wrong with her?
Sylvester	Don't ask me. Ask any incapacitated soldier in the barracks at Bannabeen. Next please?
Mickey	*(Reads on)* Dilhooley, Daisy, Crappadudeen.

Sylvester	Sounds good. Daisy Dilhooley.
Mickey	Oh she's as good as you'll get. As sure as there's meat in a butcher's shop this one is good.
Sylvester	Could it be said that's she's too good?
Mickey	Who's to say for certain. He won't do much better.
Sylvester	If he wants a ready-made heir to the throne he won't do much better.
Mickey	What are you talking about?
Sylvester	I'm talking about a slight swelling on the young lady's maw.
Mickey	Maw?
Sylvester	Maw, abdomen, stomach, belly. Call it what you will it won't bring down the swelling. Seven months gone I'd say. A dainty dame like that wouldn't be setting her cap for our man here if her figure was any way slack. What else have you? *(John places glasses on table having made the punch. He proceeds to fill them. Mickey thumbs through book. John takes a seat)*
John	Sláinte.
All	Sláinte.
Sylvester	I declare to God almighty this is a mighty brew.
Mickey	He has a way with punch.
John	I wish I had a way with women.
Mickey	A man can't have a way with everything. I had a brother could castrate bonhams blindfolded yet he couldn't put a knot in his tie.
Sylvester	Who's next?
Mickey	Drombie Delia.
Sylvester	Drombie Delia? Delia Drombie? Can't place her off hand.
Mickey	A decent sort. No chicken but nice and firm. Was going for years with a man by the name of Dan Dooley. The heart gave out on Dan a few years back and he spreading manure. These past months Delia's showing an interest in the marriage stakes again.
Sylvester	A picture is beginning to emerge. Proceed.
Mickey	One thing I'll guarantee and that is this. There was never a harness thrown across her since Dan Dooley died. *(He pours punch all round)*
Sylvester	What colour has she?
Mickey	Blonde.
Sylvester	Blonde hair?

Mickey	Blonde hair
Sylvester	Age?
Mickey	Witness can't say your honour but she's firm and she's not past it.
Sylvester	Delia Drombie, blonde ... I know her. The Lord be good to my dear departed mother. (*Crosses himself*) If she was alive today she'd by seventy-four years of age.
Mickey	What has your mother got to do with it?
Sylvester	Nothing except that she and Delia Drombie were in the same class at school. Next candidate please?
Mickey	There's only one more.
Sylvester	Last but not least eh?
Mickey	(*Reads*) Cant, Nellie, of the Tooreengarriv Cants, a perfect lady.
Sylvester	Nellie Cant?
Mickey	Know her?
Sylvester	The name has a familiar ring Nellie Cant? Can't be sure. Know her John?
John	To see. She's a Protestant isn't she?
Mickey	All the Cants are Protestants. Would you marry a Protestant John?
John	Christ Almighty man I'd marry a Mohammedan!
Sylvester	Come on. Come on. Details.
Mickey	Age thirty-one. A nice shy sort that never lifted her skirt unless it was to answer a call of nature.
John	I wish you wouldn't refer to women so crudely.
Sylvester	Why didn't she marry up to this?
Mickey	The brother, Willie Cant (*Tips his forehead*) a small bit of a want. Spent time you know where. All the poor bastard ever wanted was a woman, any sort of a woman. So I got him a woman and now the sister is free.
Sylvester	And you say she's a paragon.
John	(*To Mickey*) That she's a good-living girl. Without shadow or stain, a good-living girl. Oh yes without doubt.
Sylvester	Mickey – what's the catch?
Mickey	No catch. She's a bit odd maybe but which one of us isn't I ask you? Which one of us isn't?
Sylvester	Odd?
Mickey	A bit odd.

Sylvester	A bit odd?
Mickey	That's what I said.
Sylvester	Isn't she the same Nellie Cant that thinks she's the Black Madonna?
Mickey	Not all the time. Not all the time.
Sylvester	Of course not, not when she thinks she's Princess Margaret. Close that damn book and let's face up to reality. It looks like the spring show Johnny my lad.
Mickey	I said it all along. The spring show.
Sylvester	That's settled then.
John	Just a minute ...
Sylvester	There's just one problem.
Mickey	What's that?
Sylvester	I'm a bit short of the readies just now.
Mickey	That's no problem. John will look after that side of it. Won't you John?
John	I suppose so.
Sylvester	Good. We mustn't let the grass grow. Where's your phone?
John	In the hallway.
Sylvester	I know just the hotel. It's the ideal job for what I have in mind. *(He exits)*
Mickey	You could look happy about it.
John	I know it won't work. I'm a jinx. You know that as well as I.
Mickey	All I know is I can't help you. I seem to be out of date these past few years. As it is I'm nearly a thing of the past.
John	You tried.
Mickey	Sylvester's in touch John. You've tried it fair long enough. Time to go foul. *(Lifts his glass)* To the spring show.
John	*(Hesitant)* To the spring show. *(They lift their glasses. They clink glasses)*

(Curtain)

Link	*(John comes front)*
John	The spring show it was to be then. Another assault on the impregnable fortress of my dreams. Once more the future was bright. I hadn't a care in the world.
	(The missionaries enter, smiling and nodding and wagging a finger at John)

Ah go to hell ... I never thought of that before. I suppose some of them must end up there.
(He laughs. The missionaries look stern)
Sorry. I'll tell you what I'll do, I'll go to confession.
(The missionaries smile and exit)
That will keep them happy ... for a while.
(John goes to the confessional)

(The above is a suggested link into scene five. It helps to keep the missionaries in the action, and gives time for set change)

ACT ONE

SCENE FIVE

Action takes place in the confession box of Bannabeen parish church. Fr Kimmerley, the parish priest, is seated centre. At either side of the box a number of old people, male and female, are seated on two stools, awaiting their turns.

John Bless me father for I have sinned. It's three weeks since my last confession father. I have been drunk twice since then. Well not quite drunk, half-drunk would be nearer the truth. I had occasion to use intemperate language and took the holy name of Jesus once. I nearly had intercourse with a woman. *(Kimmerley lifts his head which had been bent the better to concentrate on what he is being told)*

Kimmerley I'm not quite sure I understand. You say you nearly had intercourse?

John That's right father. I met this woman in Cork and I nearly had intercourse with her.

Kimmerley Nearly. Would you elaborate my son?

John I was in her bedroom father. She took her clothes off ... well some of them, most of them ... and ...

Kimmerley And?

John That was all.

Kimmerley Then you didn't commit any sin.

John Didn't I?

Kimmerley Don't you know?

John I thought you'd tell me.

Kimmerley I'm only your confessor. I cannot be your conscience. We may take it that you had no sexual intercourse as such with this woman.

John As such, no.

Kimmerley Then what had you?

John Lustful designs I suppose.

Kimmerley Did you place a hand on her private part?

John No.

Kimmerley Any part of her?

John Well ... at one stage I did put my hands around her.

Kimmerley But you had no carnal knowledge?

John	No.
Kimmerley	Well, what did you do?
John	I've told you.
Kimmerley	And I don't understand.
John	I went to Cork, I met this woman we got drunk together. We went to her bedroom. She took off her clothes. She sat on the bed. I was about to take off my clothes.
Kimmerley	And then?
John	She fell asleep.
Kimmerley	Then?
John	I left.
Kimmerley	You're John Bosco McLaine aren't you?
John	For God's sake keep your voice down father.
Kimmerley	Don't worry. They can't hear you my son. Why do you unburden this saga of near conquest on me?
John	Because you're my confessor. Because I have sinned.
Kimmerley	Sinned? There isn't the makings of a dacent sin in the combined doings of all the bachelors in this parish.
John	I'm not talking about this parish I'm talking about Cork.
Kimmerley	And I'm talking about this parish because it's my parish and you're my parishioner. You're still a chastitute. There are no marriages, no births. The young girls have gone. The boys have gone after them. You and your equals are all that's left. What am I going to say to you McLaine? Should I tell you to go forth and fornicate properly and then come back so that I can give you absolution for a worthwhile sin or should I allow you decay in your own barren chastitution – or what am I to do with you at all?
John	I came here for help.
Kimmerley	I'm trying to help.
John	It doesn't sound that way.
Kimmerley	I'm being cruel to be kind, man. Can't you see that? You fellows need to be jolted, to be shocked into wakefulness. Another priest might let well alone but I can't do that.
John	All I want is absolution.
Kimmerley	It's yours with a heart and a half.
John	Give it to me and let me out of here .The crowd outside will think I'm after raping somebody.
Kimmerley	Never mind what the crowd outside think. You're on my

	conscience McLaine. I'm a down-to-earth priest. I rationalise. The Second Vatican Council should have taken parishes like this into account. Canon Law should have made special provision for the situation here where marriage is a luxury. What right have I to condemn a man who is tormented with a natural hunger for the opposite sex?
John	God's sake will you keep your voice down father.
Kimmerley	Sometimes I think the Catholic Church is blind to the real needs of places like Tubberganban where enforced chastity is stifling life itself. Three Hail Mary's and get out of my sight. *(John leaves the box. Comes front)*
John	He's a gruff old divil, Fr Kimmerley, but the heart is in the right place. And he cleaned the slate. It's a light sort of feeling you get after confession. Puts the spirit back into you. I'm in form now for the spring show, the step is light, the mind is fresh, the soul is cleansed ... and my imagination is saturated with the prospect of unlimited romance.

(CURTAIN)

Link	*(Enter John, much smartened up, by his standards)*
John	Here I am all dolled up and somewhere to go – the spring show. Me, John Bosco McLaine ... John Bosco ... I was telling you about my name some time ago but I didn't really finish. I'll tell you now. In a city a name means nothing, but in a country place like this a name like John Bosco Melchior McLaine can be a decided disadvantage. I want to make it clear that I am not against religion, but seriously don't you think the name reeks of sanctity, piety and holiness. When I was ten my father died. No he didn't die, he gave up. He allowed himself to be suffocated by repeated massive doses of rosaries and novenas. After he was buried my mother dressed in black until the day she died. She'd kneel by the door where it was draughtiest and pray for my father's soul – hours at a time, night after night. There was no need. He went straight to heaven. His hell was while he was here. I found her one morning huddled in a little heap, stone cold.

She died without a whimper. She made only two demands on her creator, my father's salvation and my virginity. Her prayers were answered on both counts. My father couldn't be anywhere else but heaven, and no one knows better than myself that I am a cock virgin, frustrated but intact. I'm the last of a species. A chastitute – which in simple language is the opposite of a prostitute. So have a good look at John Bosco McLaine, Chastitute, willing to break from his fetters, and headed for the spring show as a willing acolyte of the whoremaster Sylvester Brady.

(He is joined by Sylvester as the spring show scene lights up. Trudy and Suzanne also enter and take their place at a table)

ACT TWO

SCENE ONE

*Action takes place at spring show. Time is the afternoon. Two well-dressed, opu-
lent-looking, early middle-aged ladies are seated at a table covered with a fringed
canopy. There might be some other tables in the background. People might be seen
to pass to and fro. The ladies are served by a white-coated youth who places lib-
erally-iced drinks on the table. He accepts payment for same and withdraws or
collects empties from other tables. A number of advertisements might occupy the
area, particularly one for Sinclair's Milking Machines. This advertisement should
be the dominating feature. Enter Sylvester Brady immaculately dressed, he is followed by John Bosco who is at his brightest yet sartorially.*

Sylvester	What would you say to a drink? I'm bloody well exhausted.
John	There's a bar over there.
Sylvester	*(Looking around him shrewdly)* Let's not rush our fences. There's a likely pair.
John	They look a bit stand-offish to me.
Sylvester	They only seem like that. I'll lay odds they're the very oppo-site. Are you game?
John	I ... I ... don't know what to say.
Sylvester	Just keep your mouth shut and stick with me. *(Calls)* Bonzo, Bonzo, come here boy. Bonzooooooooo! *(He walks around search-ing for an imaginary dog. To John)* Where can he have gone to? *(He goes on all fours and looks under table. The ladies are somewhat alarmed. He lift his hat)* I beg your pardon. It's my dog. You wouldn't by any chance have seen him would you? *(The ladies are Trudy and Suzanne. Trudy the more outgoing)*
Trudy	What sort of a dog?
Sylvester	Irish wolfhound, answering to the name of Bonzo.
Trudy	*(Endeavouring to recall)* No, certainly not an Irish wolfhound. I'd have noticed. Suzanne?
Suzanne	*(Shakes her head)* No.
Trudy	Have you tried the secretary's office?
Sylvester	Not yet. Time enough for that. *(Haloos)* Here boy, here boy. *(Takes off hat)* I do beg your pardon. I should have introduced myself. My name is Sinclair. Sylvester Sinclair. Sinclair's Milk-ing Machines.

Trudy	Oh! *(Obviously impressed)*
Sylvester	This is my friend Johnny McMcNab. Flew in this morning from Australia. Johnny, say hello.
Trudy	How do you do?
John	How do you do? *(Suzanne nods)*
Sylvester	Drinks. We must have drinks. *(He raises hand and clicks fingers loudly. Immediately the same youth appears)*
Sylvester	You see to it Johnny.
John	*(To Suzanne)* What would you like?
Suzanne	Gin please, gin and tonic.
Trudy	Same for me.
Sylvester	Brandy for me. Remy Martin double with ginger ale.
John	And I'll have a small Irish.
Youth	Very good sir. *(Exit youth)*
Trudy	Won't you sit down? *(Sylvester sits near her)*
Sylvester	Sit down Johnny.
Trudy	Have you got a stand?
Sylvester	At the other end of the grounds. I'd take you there but it's so crowded. Much more pleasant here don't you think, Miss ... Eh?
Trudy	Trudy. Please call me Trudy.
Sylvester	Of course, of course. It will be Trudy ... Johnny you know. *(To Suzanne)* And you are ... ?
Suzanne	Oh ... Suzanne.
Trudy	And you Mr McNab, are you here on business?
Sylvester	He's on holiday. No business this time around. He lost his wife, poor fellow, just before Christmas.
Trudy	So sorry. Suzanne and I are widows of long-standing. We understand.
Sylvester	What a coincidence.
Trudy	And you Mr Sinclair are you married?
Sylvester	Please call me Sylvie. No, my wife alas is no longer with us. Drowned two years ago, swept over-board during a cruise.
Trudy	How terrible for you.
Sylvester	Life must go on. Isn't that what the song says? *(Youth arrives with drinks. He deposits them on table)*
Youth	Gin and tonic?
Suzanne	Thank you.
Youth	Gin and Tonic.

Trudy	Thank you.
Youth	Brandy?
Sylvester	Lay it down here boy.
Youth	Small Irish?
John	That'll be mine thank you. *(He tenders a note)* Keep the change.
Youth	Thank you sir. *(Youth withdraws)*
Sylvester	*(Lifting glass)* Cheers.
Trudy	Cheers. *(All quaff)*
Sylvester	I have a feeling we met before ... last Easter at Fairyhouse?
Trudy	No.
Sylvester	Ascot?
Trudy	Oh dear no. I've never been to Ascot.
Sylvester	Good Heavens, Bonzo – I'd forgotten all about him ... Trudy, why don't you and I try to locate the secretary's office and report the loss of my dog? *(John and Suzanne are obviously embarrassed)*
Trudy	What a marvellous idea.
Sylvester	*(Standing up)* Let's bring our drinks. *(He helps Trudy to her feet and hands her the drink. Taking his own drink he takes her arm. To John)* We'll see you later. *(Sylvester and Trudy move off. There is an uneasy silence after they go.)*
Suzanne	They're lucky with the weather.
John	They are indeed.
Suzanne	Are you staying in the city?
John	Yes. We're booked into the Elmslands.
Suzanne	We're just across the road, the Riversdale.
John	It's a small world.
Suzanne	Isn't it? *(Pause)* Are you really an Australian?
John	No. I'm not and I didn't fly in this morning either and his wife wasn't washed overboard because he never had a wife. *(Faint romantic background music)*
Suzanne	I guessed.
John	Do you mind?
Suzanne	No. Are you married?
John	No.
Suzanne	Ever?
John	Never.
Suzanne	How did you escape?
John	Maybe I tried too hard. I wanted to ... I just couldn't con any-

	body into it.
Suzanne	I don't believe that.
John	It's true, believe me. I'd have married ... any body ... I was lonely.
Suzanne	I know. I've been like that since my husband died. Do you farm?
John	Yes. I'm a farmer.
Suzanne	Have you got a girlfriend?
John	No.
Suzanne	Was there ever anybody ... important?
John	No. Not for want of effort on my part I assure you.
Suzanne	Your friend seems to have a way with girls.
John	It was he who talked me into coming to the show. I wouldn't have had the courage to come on my own. I'm lucky I suppose to have him. I wouldn't be here now talking to you if it hadn't been for him. At least I owe him that much.
Suzanne	I'm obliged to Trudy in the same way. There I was sitting by the fire bemoaning my sad fate when she breezed in and announced that we were both going to the spring show. I jumped at the chance.
John	Any family?
Suzanne	Two daughters, both married with young families. I don't fit in. I like the kids but they start to annoy me after a while. I don't seem to have the patience for children any more. When your husband dies you're cut off. It's as simple as that. But here I am talking about myself all the time. What about you? Were you ever in love?
John	You'll laugh if I tell you.
Suzanne	The last thing I'll do is laugh. Were you?
John	Several times. No. A hundred times. It never came to anything. I never even made love. I shouldn't have said that.
Suzanne	Why not?
John	I hardly know you.
Suzanne	You did say you never made love?
John	Yes
Suzanne	Why not?
John	There were times when I thought it was a sin and other times when it just didn't work out. It never does, not for me.
Suzanne	I can't believe it.

John	It's true. What an admission to have to make at my age. You'll think there's something wrong with me. I often think so myself. I've generally managed to mess up every relationship I ever had with a woman. I don't know how the hell I'm going to finish up.
Suzanne	Come on cheer up Johnny.
John	And that's another thing –
Suzanne	What?
John	My name's not Johnny. Sylvester invented that. I suppose he thought it sounded sporty. John's my name, John.
Suzanne	Very well I'll call you John. *(Puts her hand on his)* Come on, let' walk. It'll take our minds off our troubles.
John	What about the others?
Suzanne	I think Trudy will enjoy Sylvester's company better than mine.
John	And you?
Suzanne	You must have more confidence in yourself, John. Come on. *(They drift arm-in-arm across the stage. Volume of music increases)*

(CURTAIN)

Link	*(They walk front)*
John	I didn't know what she was getting at when she said that I should have more confidence in myself. It's a terrible thing when you don't know if a woman is giving you a hint or not. Anyway we walked along and she put her arm in mine and it seemed the most natural thing in the world. Now and then she caught me looking at her and she smiled. We spent the evening together and then I brought her to her hotel. We stood in the foyer and I didn't know what to say

ACT TWO

SCENE TWO

Action takes place in a hotel bedroom.

Suzanne   Would you like a drink?

John   Please.

Suzanne   It's quiet in my room. We'll have it there. *(They move into bedroom where she starts to pour drinks)* Irish Isn't it?

John   Please. *(She pours drink)* I wonder where the others are?

Suzanne   They're old enough to look after themselves. Are you worried?

John   Good God no. *(She hands him a drink)*

Suzanne   Let's drink to the future.

John   To the future. *(They quaff)*

Suzanne   Do you dance?

John   I move my legs. I doubt if you'd call it dancing.

Suzanne   You're light on your feet. You should be good on a dance floor. *(She turns on the radio. Immediately a blast of modern pop music assails their ears)* Hardly suitable for us. *(She fiddles with dial until she finds a station from which drowsy, old-time dance music can be heard, possibly the* September Song *or some such. She takes his glass)* Let's dance. *(She deposits glasses)*

John   I'll try. *(Slowly they dance to the music, she humming the melody, John still a little bewildered)*

Suzanne   Relax John. There's nobody here but ourselves. *(Slowly they dance round the room. She stops and takes his hands)* There's nothing to worry about. *(They dance again, this time cheek to cheek. They come to where drinks are. She hands him his glass, takes her own. They drink, their heads close together. She kisses him)* You finish your drink. I'll go and ... change. *(She takes coat from bed and places it across a chair. She takes negligee from underneath pillow)* Unless you don't want to.

John   I want to.

Suzanne   I won't be long. Be ready for me. *(Exit)*

John   *(To himself)* Be ready for her ... *(Suitable music playing. He takes off his shortcoat and folds it slowly and carefully. He then takes off his shoes and stockings which he places near shortcoat. He takes off* *tie and shirt. He casts it aside. He takes off trousers to reveal a pair of shorts underneath. He casts trousers aside with abandon. Is about to shed shorts when suddenly he notices two figures standing each on a dais in a corner of room. They are spot-lighted. They are the two brown-robed missionaries who used to come to Tubberganban)* Oh no. Not you two. Go away for God's sake. Why are you always haunting me? *(One of the missionaries, i.e., the cross missioner is abrasive and loud and allows himself to be carried away. The other, i.e., the quiet missioner is gentle and forbearing, never raising his voice)*

Gentle M   Ye shall be chaste above all things and ye shall be modest in dress. Ye shall not scandalise the purity of womanhood.

John   Oh God almighty what am I to do?

Cross M   There was this man, this lecher. In the tavern he plied this woman with drink upon drink. Then he took the hapless creature to his room and there he had his pleasure, his lustful animal pleasure. That night as he lay in his bed alone a sudden spasm seized him. In a moment he lay dead, dead, dead, while his blackened soul sped to hell, yes, my dear brethren, straight to hell. *(Missionaries disappear into darkness. John gropes for his trousers. Suddenly Suzanne appears in pink negligee)*

Suzanne   What's wrong John?

John   *(Distressed)* Nothing.

Suzanne   Come here John. It's all right John. Believe me it's all right. *(She takes his hands again)* You're not nervous now are you? *(John shakes his head)* You want me don't you? *(John nod his head)* Then kiss me. *(They kiss urgently and embrace. They kiss and caress seriously. Suddenly there is a deafening banging on the door. John is jolted backwards by the shock. The banging is repeated. John backs warily away from the door)* Who is it?

Voice   Open the door. Open at once.

Suzanne   But who is it? *(Deafening knocking again. Fearfully Suzanne opens the door. Enter a young uniformed porter. There is a considerable commotion in the corridor outside)* In God's name what's happening?

Porter   *(Extends arms)* Come on get out of here. There's a bomb due to go off in three minutes.

Suzanne   *(Screams)* A bomb. Oh God. A bomb. *(Screaming she runs into corridor)*

Porter	Hurry sir. It's due to go off any minute.
John	My pants. *(John gathers clothes round room)*
Porter	There's no time. *(Pushes him)* In God's name get out of here. We're the last two in the building. *(Protesting John allows himself to be rushed out)*

(CURTAIN)

Link:	*(John comes downstage wrapped in a sheet and clutching his clothes. As he speaks he dresses)*
John:	Well may you laugh. Go on. I'm getting used to it. God almighty what a disaster. Everything going so well and some eejit thinks it's a good joke to ring the hotel and say there's a bomb in the Ladies. A hoax – what would you expect with my luck. I hadn't even the satisfaction of seeing the whole bloody place blown up and myself along with it maybe. And what about Suzanne? She refused to have anything to do with me afterwards. I sent flowers to the hospital. I called several times. I met her doctor. He said it would be months before she got over the shock. Even then, he said, the sight of me would probably trigger it off again. She thinks I'm an IRA bomber. And then Sylvester turned up again with another proposition.

(CURTAIN)

ACT TWO

SCENE THREE

John moves to kitchen. Simultaneously Eva shows in Sylvester.

Eva   Mr Brady, Mr McLaine. *(With both hands Sylvester squeezes her waist from behind. She jumps forward surprised)*

Sylvester How many times must I tell you to call me Sylvie ... Now say it. Say Sylvie. Come on. Say Sylvie, say it.

Eva   Sylvie.

Sylvester All right you can go about your business. There won't be any sandwiches tonight. *(Exit Eva)*

John   Where do you get your power over women?

Sylvester Long practice my friend.

John   All right. Tell us what brought you this hour of the night?

Sylvester Pour me a drop of that brew and I'll come to the point. *(John locates glass and pours from ewer. Hands glass to Sylvester)* You've heard oul' Brewer has passed on.

John   The bookmaker?

Sylvester The very one.

John   What has Brewer's death to do with your visit here?

Sylvester I have a proposition for you.

John   *(Warily)* You have?

Sylvester With Brewer gone there's a vacancy for a bookie's shop in Bannabeen. I can muster two thousand if you put up two more. We'd be partners. After expenses we'd divide the profits down the line. What do you say?

John   Two thousand is a lot. It's not my line of business ...

Sylvester Let the business side of it to me. We can't go wrong. Just give me your cheque for two thousand and I'll have a solicitor draw up the agreement.

John   Hold it. Hold it. I have no notion of forking out two thousand pounds.

Sylvester You want her? *(Points thumb towards where Eva has exited)*

John   Who?

Sylvester Her. Eva. You want her?

John   Are you trying to make an eejit out of me?

Sylvester Have I ever failed to produce the goods for you? Have I?

111

John	No, but ...
Sylvester	It wasn't my fault if you missed the open goal. Would you have her if I got her for you?
John	Of course.
Sylvester	That's all I wanted to know. I have this damsel taped. Believe me when she's broken down there's nothing will satisfy her. Can't you see it man, the two of you sitting here watching telly across the winter. The wind howls outside. She fills your glass and her own. She sits on your lap and runs her fingers round the back of your neck. Your pulse quickens. Your heart misses a beat. She bites the bone behind your ear, a savage passionate bite. She drags you to her bedroom. I envy you. I really do.
John	When will you ask her?
Sylvester	What's wrong with right now, this very minute?
John	You think she'll listen?
Sylvester	Are you coming into partnership with me?
John	I suppose so.
Sylvester	Supposing is no good to me. Are you or aren't you?
John	You'll have to give me time to think.
Sylvester	No time. I must know now.
John	All right.
Sylvester	Good. You make tracks for the pub. Give me an hour alone with her and I'll lay the foundations. It won't be easy but I guarantee you your money's worth before the month is out. Now get out of here and let me to it.
John	All right ... you won't ...
Sylvester	I won't what?
John	Forget yourself and put your own interests before mine?
Sylvester	My plate is already full. You should know that. Now will you get out of here and let me get down to business.
John	Goodnight and good luck. *(To audience)* Of course I shouldn't have gone. I should have known better than to trust a townie. *(Exit John. When Sylvester makes certain he has indeed gone he replenishes his glass and indulges in a wholesome swallow. He then whistles briefly, sonorously and a little imperiously. Sips as he waits. Repeats whistle confidently. Eva emerges and advances coyly. Sylvester pours a dollop from ewer and hands it to her)*
Eva	Where did he take off to at this hour?

112

Sylvester	The pub.
Eva	Why didn't you go?
Sylvester	Because I promised I'd speak on his behalf.
Eva	He's a manky little runt all right.
Sylvester	I told him I'd put in a good word for him.
Eva	Don't make me laugh.
Sylvester	You can pretend can't you?
Eva	Why should I?
Sylvester	*(Puts his glass aside)* Come here, slut. *(Firmly)* I said come here. *(He flings his arms around her and kisses her expertly. They recoil when they've both had enough)* You'll be nice to your man. You lead him on. Dangle your commodities in front of him. Be so near and yet so far and we'll be sitting pretty very soon.
Eva	You take a lot for granted don't you?
Sylvester	Do I?
Eva	Yes you do. Whistling for me as if I were a bitch.
Sylvester	You came didn't you? *(Tips her under chin)* Come on. Don't be coy with me. Or maybe you want to spend the rest of your life in this wilderness.
Eva	I'm only here to put by enough for a passage to Canada.
Sylvester	That makes two of us. I have to get out. I've debts all over the place. You play your cards right and we'll be in Canada the end of the month.
Eva	You expect me to go off with you out of the blue. You have a neck you have.
Sylvester	Why don't you just shut that sexy mouth of yours and come here. *(Firmly)* Come here. *(They kiss. They embrace. Lights out)*

(CURTAIN)

ACT TWO

SCENE FOUR

The confessional at Tubberganban. A few weeks later. No array at either side this time. John at one side of confessional, elderly penitent at other. Father Kimmerley dismisses this person and turns his attention to John.

John	I am not here for confession father.
Kimmerley	Then would you mind leaving the box so that the others might be heard.
John	There are no others. I waited till they had all gone.
Kimmerley	Why are you here?
John	I have a notion father of entering Holy Orders.
Kimmerley	*(Peers)* Who have I? Don't tell me. Let me guess. It's John Bosco McLaine isn't it?
John	Correct.
Kimmerley	Now would you mind repeating yourself?
John	I said I have a notion of entering Holy Orders.
Kimmerley	So long as it remains a notion we have nothing to worry about.
John	I didn't expect you to be facetious.
Kimmerley	Sorry. Sorry. Sorry. Unintended I assure you. You see my son I am a product of Salamanca who was case-hardened in the slums of Pittsburg. The net result is that I have been turned into something of a sceptic. What precisely have you in mind?
John	The Franciscans.
Kimmerley	There is no accounting for taste. Ah well I suppose it takes all kinds to make a world. If we hadn't Franciscans I daresay we'd have some other gaggle in their stead. So you want to be a priest. What age are you?
John	I'll be fifty-three in July.
Kimmerley	And what self-respecting seminary is going to take you at that age?
John	I don't expect any problem in that respect.
Kimmerley	Oh so you just walk in with your hat in your hand and walk out a priest after a few years. Well let me tell you something.

	Without a reference from me nobody will accept you.
John	Does that mean you are witholding a reference?
Kimmerley	It does not. I'll tell you what I'll do. You come back here in three months time and if you're still serious I'll write and find out the Franciscan position regarding chaps like yourself. I'll say that as far as I know you're sound in wind and limb and have no history of mental disorder. Sure you're nearly halfway there already.
John	What do you mean?
Kimmerley	Being a chastitute is first-class preparation for celibacy.
John	I can do without sarcasm.
Kimmerley	I am not being sarcastic.
John	You're opposed to my becoming a priest?
Kimmerley	Not quite.
John	You think I'm doing the wrong thing?
Kimmerley	When all fruit fails we must try haws mustn't we?
John	I'm at a loss to understand you father.
Kimmerley	Let me ask you a question McLaine. Would certain recent events have anything to do with your decision?
John	What events?
Kimmerley	Come now the whole parish knows that your housekeeper vanished suddenly. So also did Sylvester Brady. You weren't seen sober for a week after it.
John	Do I get a reference?
Kimmerley	Come back in a month.
John	A month will be too late.
Kimmerley	As far as I can see you want to be a priest overnight.
John	And as far as I can see the only consolation for me is to go back on the booze. There's no help for me here. *(Exit John)*
Kimmerley	John, John, come back ...

(CURTAIN)

Link: John *(Appearing with a bottle of whiskey)* There are times when the only thing to do is to booze it out. Drink till you're stupefied. Sleep and try to escape. Wake up and it's all still there in front of you. More booze until you're exhausted. Then crawl back home ... And God almighty what's the first sound you hear when you open the door ...

Act Two

Scene Five

We hear the sound of the rosary as the lights come up on the kitchen. Praying are Father Kimmerley, Aunt Jane and Mickey. Enter John. The prayers stop and Aunt Jane rushes to him.

Jane	Oh John, John. God be thanked you're safe.
Mickey	Good on you boy. I knew you'd wander in some night like this.
John	Take it easy. I'm all right.
Mickey	Sit down man. Sit down.
Jane	Two weeks John and no word. I thought something terrible had happened to you.
Mickey	He was on the bottle ma'am. His bitterness had to run its course. Isn't that the way of it?
John	That's the way of it.
Kimmerley	It's good to see you John.
John	Thanks father.
Kimmerley	I feel guilty about you. You came to talk about your troubles and I didn't take you seriously. I'm sorry.
John	It wouldn't have made any difference father. I know that, and you know it too. You know where the fault is.
Kimmerley	Yes I know where the fault is, it's in every catechism in this country. And I know *what* the fault is – the fault is that men like you, John, take sex far too seriously.
Jane	What a thing to say father.
Kimmerley	It's true Miss McLaine, unfortunately.
Mickey	I'm with you all the way father. Some takes it so seriously it has them driven off their heads.
Kimmerley	It has us all driven off our heads, including myself.
Jane	Father?
Kimmerley	It's all right Miss McLaine, I have the protection of the years if not my collar.
Jane	I don't think I quite follow you father.
Kimmerley	I'm sure you don't ma'am. But if you sat in the confessional like I do you'd wonder if marital sex or single chastity caused the most trouble. Men complaining their wives are

116

	frigid, women complaining their husbands want to make prostitutes of them, and bachelors like your nephew here devouring booze to stifle the nature rising up in them.
Jane	Merciful God those are terrible words for a priest to utter. We must do as the Church teaches.
Kimmerley	That is a matter of opinion. Oh have no doubt I uphold the teachings of the Church – but my sympathy is with those who suffer.
Jane	If we allow our animal passions to get the better of us where will it all end?
Kimmerley	*(Angrily)* I'm not talking about animal passions Miss McLaine. I'm talking about sex.
Mickey	Nature must have its fling ma'am if the world is to wheel free. Isn't that it father?
Kimmerley	That's another way of putting it Mickey. I'll go now before I say too much ... Goodnight John, I'll leave you in good hands.
John	Goodnight father.
Jane	I'll see you out father.
Kimmerley	*(At door)* I'll pray for him Miss McLaine.
Jane	We'll all pray for him father.
Kimmerley	Yes. At least we owe him that much ... unless you have a better idea Mickey? *(Exit with Aunt Jane)*
	(John takes glass and Mickey fills from ewer)
Mickey	Everything will be fine from now on John. Your purgatory is behind you and there are joyful times ahead.
John	Not for me there aren't.
Mickey	Forget what happened. God never closed one door but he opened another.
John	He slammed them in my face Mickey.
Mickey	Not at all. *(Pauses)* Our friend Sylvie is gone.
John	Good riddance.
Mickey	Gone for good and glory and left a door open behind him. And left who standing there? I'll tell you who. Juleen McCoon from Tubbernaroon. *(John looks at him)* She'll be at the Crossroads dance Sunday night the same as always but this time she'll be a filly without a hobble, a filly waiting for a winkers, a filly waiting you might say to be nobbled by the right man. Or maybe you'd rather rest up awhile?

John   *(Sits upright)* No. No. I'll be all right. I'll be all right. I'll give it one more fling and that will be my last.

Mickey   You can't beat the old war-horse. All he wants is the smell of the gunpowder and he's away into the thick of the fight. Drink up John. Drink up to Sunday night and to Juleen Mc-Coon. *(They quaff)*

(CURTAIN)

Link: John *(Coming forward)* You'd think I'd have learned from past misfortunes, but no. The love buds quicken and the sap flows once more. Never say die, that's my motto. And so I gird myself once more for the onslaught. Once more to the Crossroads hopeful dance, there to sojourn and take my final chance.

ACT TWO

SCENE SIX

He enters the Crossroads pub, followed by Mickey. The usual patrons are present. The one-man band plays a tango merrily. All present dance and sing at the same time. Juleen McCoon stands near the band, cigarette in mouth, with her hands folded, tapping a foot to the beat of the tango. Mickey and John stand surveying the passing scene. Juleen lifts a hand and waves it at John. He checks to see if it's really he who is being saluted. He returns salute tentatively.

Mickey	Go on man. You're in business. She's aiming herself at you. You'd have to be blind not to notice. Go on.
John	You prophesied correctly. She's here and she seems willing.
Mickey	There's no obstacle in your way tonight. Off you go, she won't wait forever. *(John goes hesitantly. Juleen joins him sultrily. She sweeps him off his feet and dances him around. The music stops. They come back to the table)* Well now it must be said, because it would be a shame not to say it, I never saw such a well-matched couple on a dance floor. Tis like ye were made for one another.
Juleen	He brings out the best in me.
John	It's the other way around. I couldn't dance to keep myself warm.
Juleen	You're too modest. That's what's wrong with you.
Mickey	Sit and I'll get you a drink. A whiskey for you John. And what about yourself Miss?
Juleen	I'll take the same as Johnny here. *(Juleen gently pushes John onto chair, then sits on his lap. She takes his glass and holds it to his mouth. He sips, she sips)* Are you comfortable?
John	Oh yes.
Juleen	Am I too heavy for you?
John	Oh God no.
Juleen	Are you sure? *(Mickey returns with drinks)*
Mickey	He was never so sure of anything in his life. Were you John?
John	True Mickey, true. Never so sure. *(The music starts. Juleen jumps to her feet as the strains of a tango are heard)*
Juleen	Come on Johnny ... I hate to miss a dance. You won't be exhausted will you?

Mickey   Look at him, if there's anyone exhausted before this night's out it'll be yourself girl. *(They dance. Mickey is delighted)*

One-Man Band: Thank you ladies and gentlemen. The next dance will be a ladies' choice. Please take your partners for a tango. *(Appropriate tango music. Juleen and John lead the floor. They are followed by other couples. Juleen dances the lead, taking long steps John vainly tries to keep in touch. Suddenly a Travolta-like townie enters. He is followed by two thuggish satellites. He takes his cigarette from his mouth, tops it and places butt in lower inside coat pocket. He bears down on John and Juleen. He taps John on shoulder. John turns round)*

Townie   Excuse me. *(He takes Juleen in his arms and sweeps her out of John's reach to the delight of his friends. John stands foolishly watching the dancing pair. They come his way. He taps townie on shoulder. Townie stops. Music stops)* Yes?

John   Excuse me. *(John goes about taking Juleen in his arms but he is firmly taken by the collar and pulled backwards by townie whose friends move menacingly forward)*

John   You excused me. I have the same right to excuse you.

Townie   But it isn't an excuse-me. It's a ladies' choice.

John   The lady happened to choose me.

Townie   Is that so?

John   Before you came in.

Townie   Exactly. Before I came in. But now I'm in and you're out. The lady has chosen me.

John   No she hasn't.

Townie   Why don't you ask her?

John   I'm not afraid of you Mister whoever you are.

Townie   Ask the lady.

John   Is it to be me or him?

Juleen   Why don't you go home? There's nothing here for you.

John   So that's the way is it. I should have known better. *(Townie gently pushes Juleen to one side. He raises his fists. John raises his. The two satellites move in from behind and beat John to the ground. He rises and is helped by Mickey whose help he spurns. He staggers out into the night. The dance resumes. Business as usual)*

(CURTAIN)

Act Two

Scene Seven

Action takes place in kitchen.

John   Damn him. Damn the townie. Damn all townies. There should be a union in every parish in this country to keep out townies. Dammit, we countrymen should be first served in the event of there being certain merchandise on the market, if you know what I mean. *(His imagination works. Enter Sylvester and two girls. They circle him)* Strong measures should be taken to control these bucks from towns and cities. They should be deprived of their vital organs and these should be transfixed on telegraph poles and piers of gates as a warning to all would-be seducers from outside the area. *(Behind him, the trio laugh, and exit up-stage)* Go away. Go away. *(Shouts after them)* Go to hell. *(Enter two missioners)*

Cross M   Hell.

Gentle M   Hell.

Cross M   Hell.

John   Oh God. Oh my God. You might say it all began with those two missioners. I'll never forget the way their robes billowed like sails when they scoured the parish for confession dodgers and assorted transgressors. *(As he talks Juleen and townie walk into view with arms around each other)*

Missioners *(Sing)* Faith of our fathers holy faith,
    We will be true to thee till death.
    O how our hearts beat high with joy!

John   My heart didn't beat high with joy. It beat high with terror at the thought of hell.

Cross M   Are you prepared to roast in hell's fire for all eternity in exchange for one moment of animal passion?

John   For pity's sake I never had one moment of any kind of passion. That's what has me the way I am.

Cross M   There is no outrage more hateful to God, as when a man made in God's likeness lures an innocent girl along the road to damnation.

John   If you think all young girls are innocent you're a fool.

Cross M	Do you think God is a fool? Do you? Do you?
John	No.
Gentle M	*(Organ music)* Take your beads in your hands and repeat after me. I will be true to my Catholic faith. I will shun the society of those who lead me into evil ways. I will never sin with a woman.
John	Shut up. Shut up. What right have you to dictate to me? Is Holy Ireland right and the rest of the world wrong? Why were me and my unfortunate equals chosen above other races to preserve our virginity as if it were a scared relic? Why us? Why?
All	Virgin most pure.
John	You took away my dignity. Without my dignity I am nothing.
All	Virgin most chaste.
John	You made me feel ashamed.
All	Tower of Ivory.
John	A man can have a woman without shame almost anywhere on earth except in this insane place.
All	Refuge of sinners.
	Queen conceived without original sin. Queen of peace. *(Women laugh at him)*
John	*(Takes gun)* Look at them. Look at them. They haunted me all my life – missioners, townies, women – most of all women. I'll never get away from them. Except one way. I'm going to blow my brains out while I still have some shred of dignity left, while I still resemble in some way the man I'm supposed to be. So here goes and they can say what they like about me when I'm gone. *(Raises gun)* No. I've a better idea! *(Fires, laughs)* Yes, I've a better idea. Why should I do it suddenly with a gun when this way is just as sure. *(Indicates punch)* It will take a bit longer but it's just as sure and who is to say whether it's a sin or not? It's not suicide. I'll fox them, by God I'll fox them. They don't know the crying loneliness of nights without end, the barrenness of summer days when all the world is singing, but me, that has no note left to join in. A toast! *(Lifts bottle)* To the end of loneliness and pain, and of John Bosco McLaine, who died for want of love.

CURTAIN

MANY YOUNG MEN OF TWENTY
TWENTY
A Bar-Room Sketch

Many Young Men of Twenty was first presented in 1961 by the Southern Theatre Group at the Father Mathew Hall, Cork with the following cast:

Peg Finnerty	Siobhán O'Brien
Danger Mulally	James N. Healy
Maurice Browne	Michael Twomey
Seelie Hannigan	Abbey Scott
Tom Hannigan	Dan Donovan
Maynan	Kay Healy
Dawheen Timmineen Din	Tom Vesey
Kevin	Flor Dullea
Dinny	Bernard Power
Kitty Curley	Mary O'Donovan
Dot	Irene Comerford
J. J. Houlihan	Bob Carlile
Johnny	Donal Farmer
Aloysius	Charles Ginnane
Mikey	Ian Halligan
Mary	Geraldine McDonald

The play was produced by Dan Donovan, with settings by Frank Sanquest.

TO PEG AND JOHN
WITHOUT WHOSE ASSISTANCE I COULD NOT POSSIBLY BE SO LATE ON FIRST NIGHTS.

ACT ONE

Action takes place in the back room of a village public-house, somewhere in southern Ireland.

There are appropriate advertisements hanging from the walls. Two tables occupy the room, one large and one small. There are several chairs and a bench.

A man and a woman sit at larger table; a girl in her early twenties at the smaller one. They are completing breakfast, backs to each other.

The man is Tom Hannigan. The woman is his sister Seelie. The girl is Peg Finnerty.

Tom Hannigan is coatless, smoking a cigarette. He is fortyish. Seelie is slightly younger, severe, sits rigidly and is outwardly composed. Peg Finnerty is young, pretty and dressed poorly.

The time is the morning of a summer's day. It is the present time.

Seelie	*(Precise, correct)* What time is it?
Tom	*(Alerted)* Almost half-ten; nearly time to open.
Seelie	Yes; there should be a few going to England.
Tom	Ah, well *(Rises)* … I'll open the front door. We should have a few before the train. *(Tom opens front door. A tattered but respectable figure stands outside)* Oh, it's you, Aloysius. First to the door as always. The usual, I suppose? *(Aloysius nods and sits)*
Seelie	*(Rising)* You brush and tidy up here, Peg. I'll take the ware to the back kitchen. *(Seelie finds a basin under table and proceeds to fill it with the breakfast things. Peg rises and exits to left, briefly, returning with brush)* Watch what he's doing!
Peg	Who?
Seelie	Who do you think …?
Peg	I'll watch him. *(Peg commences to brush floor towards direction of fireplace at right)*
Seelie	You'll get a cloth, Peg, and shine the place up a bit and … *(Meaningly)* you remember what I told you about himself … if you see him nippin' at the bottles, be sure and tell me.
Peg	Yes, Miss Seelie! *(Exit Seelie by door near fireplace. Peg continues with her brushing and commences to sing)* Many young men of twenty said goodbye

	All that long day
	From break of dawn until the sun was high
	Many young men of twenty said goodbye.
	My boy, Jimmy, went that day
	On the big ship sailed away
	Sailed away and left me here to die
	Many young men of twenty said goodbye.
	(Peg continues to hum the air. Tom enters cautiously)
Tom	Is she gone?
Peg	She's probably washin' the ware. She told me to keep an eye on you.
Tom	Good! *(He exits hastily)*
Peg	*(Singing)*
	My Jimmy said he'd sail across the sea
	He swore his oath
	He'd sail again, back home to marry me
	My Jimmy said he'd sail across the sea
	But my Jimmy left me down
	O, my Jimmy, please come back to me!
	O, my Jimmy, please come back to me!
	(Peg sings the song again. Tom enters, head craned forward first, hands behind back. He walks forward towards fireplace and produces a tumbler of whiskey from behind his back)
Tom	*(To Peg)* You won't say a word about this?
Peg	No!
Tom	*(Surveys whiskey)* 'Twas never needed more, Peg! *(Swallows whiskey – sighs contentedly)* Ah, good God, there's a great rattle in that! *(Tom shakes his shoulders. Enter Seelie suddenly. Tom just manages to get the glass into his trousers pocket)*
Seelie	Why aren't you in the bar?
Tom	*(A little flustered)* Checkin' up! Just checkin' up!
Seelie	Come here at once! *(Tom goes towards her)* Come on, puff! *(Tom extends his head and blows his breath on to her face. Immediately she slaps his face. She turns to Peg)* You … You … Don't you know what he's doin' to himself? I thought I told you to tell me? I should have known what to expect from you … a tramp!
Tom	Peg knew nothing about it. She didn't see me.
Seelie	Taking sides against me! … Listen to me, Tom Hannigan. If you touch another drop of that bottle today, you can be ready

	to leave here ... and I mean it, this time! *(Rousing herself)* How long do you think I'm going to take it from you? Every night when you go to bed, you're drunk ... stupid drunk. You think I don't hear you staggerin' against the sides of the stairs and missin' every other step?
Tom	'Twas only a little drop to cure myself after the night. I'd a shake in my hand.
Seelie	It's the same every morning. I'm not taking any more of it, Tom, and I'm not warnin' you any more either. *(She exits)*
Tom	A wonderful start to the day. *(Takes the glass from his pocket)* She knocked all the enjoyment out of it. How do you stick it here at all, Peg? Why don't you pack your traps and head away for England?
Peg	I can't go.
Tom	If 'tis the money, Peg ... I have some. I often thought to make a break of it myself, but sure she'd have no one to give out to if I went.
Peg	She's your sister, Tom. I'm only the servant girl here. All she has is you, Tom.
Tom	Forget about her! Do you want money?
Peg	'Tisn't the money. Sure I couldn't go without the little fellow.
Tom	He'll be all right with your father and mother. You'll never do any good for yourself here. I see you there often, Peg, when lads walk into the bar outside, especially them travellers with motor-cars, an' they all trying to get off with you ...

(From without the door on the wall facing audience, from a distance, can be heard the voice of a man singing. Aloysius rises and departs at the sound)

Voice	*(Singing)*
	Oh, rise up, Mikey Houlihan, 'tis you're the dauntless man, When Ireland, she was in her woe, you was always in the van. Near to the town of Keelty, you were murdered in July; God rest you, Mikey Houlihan, the darlin' Irish boy.
Peg	*(In the middle of the singing)* That's Danger Mullaly comin'!
Tom	With a sick head as usual, an' short four pence for the price of a pint. *(Enter Danger Mullaly. He is fiftyish, tattered, curious. His accent is semi-detached and varied and stentorian. He carries a timber box, painted red, in his hand. The box is a foot square and about three inches high, it is tied around his neck. He enters by door on*

wall facing audience)

Danger *(To no one in particular)* 'Oh, rise up, Mikey Houlihan, that brave and dauntless boy ...' Mikey Houlihan! Mikey boloney! Shot by accident for Ireland. Twenty-four of his relations drawing state pensions and twenty-four more in government jobs, and here am I, Danger Mullaly, with my box full of holy pictures an' short four pence on the price o' the pint. *(Changes tone to intimacy)* 'Tis frightful quiet, Peg Finnerty, for a mornin' before the train. 'Tis frightful quiet, Tom Hannigan. *(Puts his box on the table)* That's the lookin' they have at me! You'd swear I was the solicitor that advised Pontius Pilate ... *(Changes tone)* Tom Hannigan, as sure as there's brown bastards in China, I'll pay you the extra four pence ... here's a shillin' on the table, a silver shillin', made an' manufactured by tradesmen that had a feelin' for beauty ... proposed, passed and seconded herewith ... one pint of Guinness for a sick man ... balance to be paid in due course on the word of Danger Mullaly, guilty but insane ... *(Pause)* Guinness, a porter-maker that had his face on a stamp the same as Parnell.

Tom What'll we do with him, Peg?

Peg *(Now dusting about room)* I'm not speakin' to him! Don't ask me!

Tom It's lookin' bad, Danger!

Danger *(Dignity)* Peg Finnerty, I know you love me ... so does many a young girl in this locality and away unto parts west. I can't marry ye all an' besides I had a letter yesterday from a doctor's daughter in Knocknagoshel that she might have an heir for the throne.

Peg *(Laughing)* Give him the pint, Tom!
(Exit Tom shaking head. Danger sits, dignified, on chair. Peg continues to sing, pausing from her dusting when she reaches the line: 'I knew I bore ...' then she goes on)
The dawn was fledged upon the mountain's rim
The day he went
I knew I bore the livin' child of him;
I knew I bore the livin' child of him;
And the child was born to me
Jimmy's gone across the sea
The dawn is dead upon the mountain's rim

	Here I wait for word of my love, Jim.
Danger	Why do you be always singin' that oul song? Where did you pick it up, anyway?
Peg	*(Absently)* The song suits me! Did you know I was called to a training college for teachers once, years ago? My father an' mother couldn't imagine that their daughter might be a teacher, an' they couldn't pay.
Danger	Oh … so that's it! … because you had a bit o' misfortune, you're goin' to be chantin' like an ordained parish clerk for the rest of your life? *(Loudly)* You had a baby … sure, you're not the first an' you won't be the last. What about it? You've a figure for fun an' frolickin', an' you're as handsome as ever stood or l'id. 'Tis hardly a monkey you'd have! Who in the parish o' Keelty is better designed an' moulded for such things? Divil the one! Sure, there's no children at all be born here, only divils that carry stories an' the twins of spite an' bitterness, an' do you know who their fathers an' mothers are? You don't … I'll tell you, Peg Finnerty. Mr Jealous and Mrs Ignorance, an' you're grumblin' with a fine bonny boy with limbs as supple as a cat an' a grin on his dial like a drake in the rain … *(Triumphant)* Didn't you give birth?
Peg	*(Impulsively touches his arm)* Oh, you're a treasure, Danger! You always cheer me up! God bless you! But I know you're lookin' for a pint and that you'd rise me up to the moon if you thought I'd stand one. My hard-bought experience says blow, blow, Danger!
Danger	*(Jumps up, in false pride)* My one boast is that I'm the greatest liar an' the biggest sinner in the parish o' Keelty an' now you're tryin' to deprive me o' my natural rights by tellin' me that I'm a treasure. *(Enter Tom with a pint of Guinness which he places on table. Danger surveys the pint from various angles)* A very knowledgeable man, the man that filled that; A man that knows his oats. A very … very … *(Sings)*

Oh, rise up, Mikey Houlihan, the brave and dauntless man
For when you ate black puddings, sure you used no frying pan
You fought for Ireland's glory and there's no one can deny
You filled up English factories with many an Irish boy.

(Seizes pint and quaffs most of it, grins and relaxes) I see a pony-load of mountainy cawbogues untacklin' in the yard when I

	was comin' in.
Tom	I suppose a few lads hittin' for England ... Did you know 'em?
Danger	I have no truck with that mountainy crew. They'd sell the britchin' o' St Joseph's ass.
Tom	I wonder who from the mountains is goin' across the water tonight?
Peg	Don't ask me! I'm in the other side o' Keelty.

(Danger sups pint, replaces same, and surveys its diminishing content)

Danger	Here they are now!

(Door on wall facing audience opens and a procession of four enters: No. 1 is Dawheen Timmineen Din. No. 2 is his wife Maynan. No. 3 is his son Kevin. No. 4 is his son Dinny. Dinny and Kevin carry a heavy suitcase each. Dawheen Timmineen Din is a weary, crafty man of sixty with cap pulled down over shrewd eyes. Dressed in country fashion he wears a gansey zipped to throat and carries a whip and trap cushions in his hand. He places these in the corner while the trio wait behind him)

DTD	*(To Tom – slow tough speech, ingratiating yet domineering)* Would there be any chance you'd get some one to throw a quarter stone of oats to the pony.
Peg	I'll do it! *(Peg exits. DTD with a motion of his hand orders his people to occupy kitchen)*
Tom	Sit down, let ye! Are the two lads for England? *(DTD sits)* You're Dawheen Timmineen Dinny, aren't you?
DTD	*(Occupying seat)* That's right!

(His wife Maynan wears a long black shawl over blouse and skirt. She sits near her husband. Kevin and Dinny wear new suits. They deposit their suitcases out of the way and sit together awkwardly. Kevin is the older and taller. Dinny seems to lean towards Kevin for protection. They would be about 25 and 18)

Tom	What will I be gettin' for ye?
DTD	Is your clock right?
Tom	Right by the church clock.
DTD	What time is it now?
Tom	*(Looks through left door into bar)* Ten to eleven.
DTD	What would that leave us for the train?
Tom	A half an hour with a few minutes to spare.

DTD	*(Nudges wife)* What'll you sample?
Maynan	Have they port wine?
DTD	Give us a port wine, a whiskey for myself and give the boys two bottles o' minerals.
Kevin	Give me a pint o' stout … D'you want one, Dinny?
	(Dinny looks anxiously at his father)
DTD	A half whiskey, a half o' port wine, *(viciously)* a pint and a bottle o' minerals. *(Singing)*

When you go to London town, work like Maggie May
Like Mikey Joe, send home the dough
Let no week pass without your father's fiver.
Rise at first light, stay home at night,
And never ate black pudding of a Friday.

Kevin/Dinny: *(Singing)*

We'll do all the things you say
We'll work day and night.
On each pay day we'll kneel and pray
And send our poor old father home his fiver
And we declare, we hereby swear
We'll never ate black puddin's of a Friday.

(Tom, exiting, repeats order to himself. Danger husbands his pint and surveys newcomers arrogantly)

DTD	*(Addressing his sons)* Ye know what's before ye over there. 'Twill be a great change for well-reared foolish young country lads. Ye'll see doxies with dyed heads cockin' their dresses high in the air, an' exposin' fair amounts o' thigh to entice the innocent young garsúns; trickers an' twisters of all sorts persuadin' you the sun was the moon; whiskery looberas with silvery tongues speech-makin' from timber boxes …
Maynan	An' eatin' black puddin's on a Friday!
DTD	Ye'll hear thunderin' black-hearted buckos at every street corner in the city o' London callin' God away from His sky, an' threatenin' people with the end o' the world.
Maynan	There's a frightful test before ye. Keep to yeerselves an' to yeer brothers an' sisters over. Call every stranger ye meet 'Sir'! an' look as foolish as ye can, an' praises in all be to the Holy Mother o' God, ye'll be a credit to yeer father an' mother.
Danger	*(Advances with his red box)* Will ye buy a picture of the Sacred Heart, three pence the piece, to be hung up, with a thumb tack

thrown in. I sold four already this mornin' to four beautiful girls goin' over workin' in factories. *(He is ignored)* Have I some class of a disease, or are ye gone deaf? *(Turns to Kevin and Dinny)* What about the two of ye? Ye'll be wantin' a Sacred Heart to pin up over the bed when ye go across.

DTD 'Tis little enough money them two has!

Danger *(Piously, sanctimoniously, to ceiling)* O, Holy High Heaven! *(Latinish twist)* O, Sanctimonii Gazulio! *(As if he were addressing a judge)* How many sons is he sending to England today? … *(Counts)* One! … Two … *(To himself)* Two! … How many has he there before? … Approximately seven with daughters included. A wise investment. *(To the two boys)* Did he tell ye to send home a pound or two every week to your poor father and mother? Did he tell ye not to forget the starvin' couple at home, rearin' what's left of ye? *(Kevin and Dinny exchange glances)* Did he tell ye the trouble he has to make ends meet an' how his bones are fettered with hunger from shortages of money an' the deadly struggle he had supportin' ye? Take a good look, boys, at yeer Da and Ma! Is there a tear on their faces? Is their hearts broke? Did ye ever in all the shortness of yeer lives see such a brace of dog-bucketin', cat-huntin', cantankerous curiosities? … *(Completely changes tone and addresses Kevin)* Stand us an oul' pint, young fella!

Kevin Right! Wait till he comes in with the drinks.

(Danger, quaffs remainder of his pint, and places glass in Kevin's hand)

DTD 'Tis little enough money you have without buyin' pints for bar bums in the village o' Keelty!

Danger *(Squarely addressing DTD)* I know all about you!

DTD *(Nettled)* Me! You don't even know the name that I'm called by.

Danger Don't I? Not that it makes any odds! *(Screws his head upwards in thought; then in sparsely divided bursts)* Mountainy farmer, chickens twenty, cows six, dogs two, wife one. Misery. *(Pause)* Sons numerous. Daughters too. All departed. House of grumblin'. House of arguin'. Dawheen Timmineen Din!

DTD That's my name!

Danger An' your grandfather, Din, was no joke! 'The Blocker' they called him on account of he blockin' a cross-eyed doxy on a

132

grave-mound in the churchyard o' Keelty.

(DTD fumes and engages his wife in furious whispers. Enter Tom Hannigan bearing tray with drinks)

Tom *(Plausibly)* Now! A half a port … *(Hands it to Maynan)* a half a whiskey. *(Hands it to DTD. Tom hands pint to Kevin and Orange-juice to Dinny)*

DTD What's goin' to you?

Tom Five an' tuppence for the drinks. *(Carefully DTD extracts five shillings and two pence and hands it to Tom)*

Tom And two an' tuppence more for the oats.

DTD Oats! *(Regretfully finds additional money and hands same over)* Oats are an awful price by you!

Tom They're scarce! *(Accepts money)*

Kevin Bring in a pint to this man. *(Indicating Danger. Tom takes Danger's empty glass and exits)*

Danger Danger Mullaly is the name, sir. 'Danger' on account of my red box with my holy pictures. *(Impulsively thrusts pictures at Kevin and Dinny. Then, on a whim, gives one to DTD and one to Maynan)* Fair due is my policy. *(To Kevin)* What part of England are ye bound for?

Kevin London.

Danger A great spot! A fella was tellin' me he saw a five-acre garden of cabbage from the train going into it. They must ate a sight of cabbage there. What sort o' work will ye be fallin' into?

Kevin The brother is foreman in a factory there. He has jobs got for us.

Danger I hope ye'll have every day's good luck. *(Enter Tom with Danger's pint. Kevin pays him. Danger accepts pint and Tom exits)* 'Tis a sin to drink it! *(Swallows deeply)*

DTD *(Rises)* I can't be wastin' my day in a public-house. 'Tis warm weather an' there's the milk o' six cows for the creamery. *(A little kindly)* Ye know the way to the station? *(Kevin nods)* Well, safe journey! *(Shakes hands with both sons, obviously embarrassed at the contact)* Say goodbye to your mother. *(Goes towards street exit, having collected his belongings)* An don't be lookin' over the side o' the ship for fear one of ye might fall into the salt water. *(Exit Dawheen Timmineen Din, followed by the amazed stare of Danger Mullaly)*

Danger If I hadn't seen and heard it with my own two eyes, I would

	not believe it. That man has a flagstone for a heart. *(Danger retreats a little as Maynan approaches her sons)*
Maynan	*(Shakes Kevin's hand)* Don't forget yeer prayers an' the three Hail Marys for purity an' a happy death. Tell your brother Padna that Juleen is for Confirmation next month, an' 'tis time he sent home a few pounds – that his father said it. *(Takes Dinny's hand)* Mind yourself, Dinny, an' don't be wanderin' off on your own. Stand close to Kevin on the boat an' you'll come to no harm. The grace o' God an' His Blessed Mother go with ye. I have the holy water here with me. Katty Fitzgerald brought it from Lourdes. *(She produces small bottle filled with water and pours some on her fingers, sprinkles it on her sons and crosses herself as the boys do. On second thoughts she sprinkles some on Danger. Enter Peg Finnerty)*
Peg	Your husband said to hurry on, Mrs Din, or the milk'd be gone sour in the tank at home! *(Maynan corks bottle and conceals it, gently touches the heads of both boys, then turns to go)*
Dinny	*(Weakly)* Ma … !
Maynan	*(Turns briefly, quietly)* What Dinny? *(He suddenly takes both her hands and begins to sob into them. She draws away after a second and, at door, turns)* Mind him, Kevin! He's only a child! *(Exit Maynan. Dinny continues to sob childishly. Kevin buries his head in his hands for a moment, then, realising where he is, defensively sits upright, and puts his arm about Dinny)*
Kevin	*(Gently)* Don't cry, Dinny … Don't be lonely … we'll be home again soon and sure, won't I be with you the whole time an' won't you be meetin' all the lads over? … Your own brothers an' sisters … they'll be all waitin' at Euston. We'll be home again for a holiday in a year. Sure a year is no length of time, man! *(Dinny continues to cry. Very gently)* Now, Dinny! 'Tisn't so bad. *(Near to tears himself, Danger turns away. Peg Finnerty occupies herself with dusting)* Don't be cryin', Dinny, or you'll have me cryin' too an' 'twould never do to have the two of us be cryin'. Sure you won't be cryin', Dinny? Think o' the journey before us an' all the new things we'll see an' the fine time we'll have when we meet the lads. Do you know what we'll do, Dinny – the two of us'll get blithero on the boat goin' over and join up with a sing-song … Won't you stop cryin' now,

	Dinny … for me, Dinny?

(Dinny sniffles and Kevin immediately gives him his handkerchief)

Dinny	I'm sorry, Kev … I'm ashamed o' myself!
Kevin	Don't be sorry, Dinny. I understand. If you didn't cry I'd have started myself.
Dinny	I want to go out a minute, Kev … I don't want to go away at all, Kev.
Kevin	I'll take you out.
Danger	Stay as you are! I'll take him out! *(Danger assists Dinny to exit)* That one there is makin' eyes at you all the time. I seen her.
Peg	Go on out, or I'll fire the pint at you! *(Exit Danger and Dinny)* That oul' devil! He's always makin' up things.
Kevin	He's a gas old man.
Peg	Your brother is awful lonesome goin'!
Kevin	So would you be lonesome, too, if you were goin'!
Peg	Don't tell me that a big boy like you is goin' to be lonesome, too?
Kevin	Everyone is lonesome at leavin' home.
Peg	Usen't I see you a few years back at the dances at Fahera Cross?
Kevin	We used often go there. I used to take Dinny. I never remember seein' you, though!
Peg	Ah, I used be dressed up that time. Anyway, you'd be too young.
Kevin	*(Laughs)* Sure, I'm away older than you!
Peg	*(Seriously)* I was too grown up, maybe. *(Changes tone)* You're a nice fella, the way you minded Dinny.
Kevin	Some one had to mind him.
Peg	Danger'll tell him a fistful o' lies now. He's a great warrant to cheer a person up.
Kevin	'Tis strange, I don't remember you at all at Fahera dance hall.
Peg	Sure, I told you I was all dressed up in them days.
Kevin	Still I should remember you.
Peg	D'you remember Jimmy Farrelly, the teacher's son, that used play the football?
Kevin	I do well! I often saw him playin'. He was goin' to the university. He ran away from home, or somethin'.
Peg	He ran away all right! D' you remember the lady he used have dancin' with him, the one with all the fancy steps.

Kevin	I do, well! She was the best-lookin' girl in Fahera dance hall. I was often half tempted to ask her for a dance but I was afraid.
Peg	*(Knowledgeable)* Oh, he'd let no one dance with her!
Kevin	I wasn't afraid of him! I was afraid of her! She'd knock you down with the good looks she had.
Peg	Would you know her if you saw her again?
Kevin	I'd know her anywhere!
Peg	You would, would you? ... Well – have a good look!
Kevin	*(Looks at her curiously)* God in Heaven! ... You don't look ... Japers! ... You are!
	(Peg places hand on hip, raises other over head, permitting her fingers to delicately touch head)
Peg	Remember now?
Kevin	That's right! That's the way you used to dance all right. *(Stands up)* Jimmy Farrelly would stand back from you and clap his hands, an' you'd swing away dancin' on your own around the floor. *(Kevin commences to clap his hands while Peg commences a modern dance. When she completes a circle or two around the room, she throws herself backwards on to a chair)* You can still dance!
Peg	If Miss Seelie saw me now, I was sacked on the spot.
Kevin	That was good dancin'. *(He sits down)*
Peg	I don't know what made me do it. I couldn't help it. I suppose there's a kick in me yet in spite of all my misfortune.
Kevin	God, you were great! It brought me back to Fahera dance hall and the innocent times I had. Myself an' Dinny! Myself an' Dinny, we'd have gay times there. We often saw a few ladies home. Where did your man Jimmy Farrelly go to?
Peg	*(Sadly)* I don't know ... he disappeared one mornin'. That night we had a date for the pictures here in Keelty an' he never came. I waited for four hours. He knew there was somethin' wrong.
Kevin	Did you ever hear from him since?
Peg	Never!
Kevin	I suppose you were in love with him?
Peg	I was.
Kevin	How is it you never chanced to come out to the dance hall since?
Peg	Are you tryin' to grig me by any chance?

Kevin	No, indeed!
Peg	You mean you don't know about me?
Kevin	As God is my judge, I don't *(Passionately)* … an' I'm not griggin' you either.
Peg	*(Stands suddenly upright and looks into fireplace)* I had a baby!
Kevin	Oh, you married since, so, did you?
Peg	*(Viciously but without intent)* No, I did not marry! I had a child out o' Jimmy Farrelly an' my own foolishness an' fancy steps. Don't look so sorry for me. I'm able to manage my affairs.
Kevin	*(Regaining his composure)* I'm not sayin' a word to you.
Peg	*(Defensively)* An' you don't have to. I know what's in your head, the same as every other fella that comes in here half drunk. They know I made a mistake an' they think on that account I'm a bit of an ape an' they all want me to go to a dance or a picture, thinkin' to have a night's sport outside.
Kevin	I'm not half-drunk … an' I'm sorry for what happened to you. Where's the child?
Peg	At home with my father an' mother. *(Brusquely)* I didn't mean to lose my temper with you. I couldn't help it. *(Pitifully)* I made one mistake an' I'm suppose to remember it for the rest of my life!
Kevin	*(Appealingly)* I'm awful sorry.
Peg	Here's in your brother, with Danger.
Kevin	Would it be all right if I wrote to you when I got over?
Peg	Oh, don't be coddin' me, boy!
	(Enter Dinny, followed by Danger)
Danger	By the Jingoes! There was enough eggs in his belly to journey to the moon. *(Dinny sits near Kevin, who takes his hand in his. To pint)* Did you miss me, my little black sweetheart? *(Swallows some)* My little black woman that I love! *(Suddenly, to Kevin and Dinny)* A word of advice about London. Marry two black women if ye can. *(Some laughter from Peg and Kevin)* There's rumours that the sweat off a black woman would cure any class of an ache or disease. There's some kind of oil in 'em. And about holy water; don't ever ask an Englishman for holy water, because he'll say "Oly Wot?"
	(Enter Tom, hands carrying glass of whiskey behind his back)
Tom	*(Customary ultimatum)* There's only a quarter of an hour left for the train. *(He walks forward to fire and puts his back to it)*

Dinny	Time we were goin', Kevin!
Danger	'Tis only two minutes walk. There's no use in ye standin' above with every hairy molly in the village o' Keelty watchin' ye.
Tom	Good luck! *(Tom quaffs glass of whiskey and puts glass in his trousers pocket. Enter Seelie)*
Seelie	*(To Tom – pointing at Danger)* I thought it was understood that he was barred here?
Tom	*(Falsetto – to Danger)* Come on! Come on! Finish that drink, an' out with you! We can't have this kind o' thing goin' on.
Danger	Oh, but excuse me! *(To Seelie)* These two boys contracted with me to bring their bags to the train. This dacent boy here stood me a pint. Am I goin' to renege on my word?
Seelie	When I think of the hard-workin' poor men with families an' watch your idleness, it makes my heart twist an' turn like a snipe. Every mornin' it's the same. You come in here on the bum. How can these poor boys afford to be buyin' you porter. What have they but the bare few shillings to spare? How is it always the poor people you fasten on?
Danger	Hang the poor! Damn the poor! Blast the poor! Why should I give a dog-bucketin' damn about the poor? What good are they? When they have a bit o' money it burns holes in their pockets. Down with the poor! Dance on 'em! Keep them down! That's my policy. The poor, how are you? Sheep dogs – that's what the poor are – trained, tamed sheep dogs. I seen lads like these before in this very pub an' they hittin' the highroad for England, lonesome stinkin' sheep dogs. Then they come back with new suits an' fancy shirts, with tall tales about loose women in Piccadilly, boastin' an' braggin' about all the money they're earnin'. Fine mannerly accents like a country curate at his first sermon. Men o' the world, with stories about the wonderful sights o' Camden Town. They'll buy porter for me when they come back on their holidays. They'll buy porter for any one. They'll buy porter for every smart man that'll believe their stories. I'm only an oul' bum! I know that! I'm only Danger Mullaly with my Sacred Hearts! I'll watch hundreds o' 'em goin' back again till the summer's over – back to their night shifts, an' filthy digs an' thievin' landladies. I'll be lookin' at them with their long faces leanin' out o' the carriage win-

	dows, with all their hard-earned money gone, an' their hearts broke with the thoughts of what's waitin' over. *(To Kevin and Dinny)* 'Tisn't so bad this time. This time it's an adventure. But wait till ye'll be goin' back the next time an' the time after that an' the time after that again. 'Twon't be an adventure then. *(Pitch of indictment)* But I don't blame you two misfortunes … *(Indicates departed father and mother)* I blame them – yeer fathers and yeer mothers. They take the easy way out. England is there or America is there. Ship 'em off an' we'll be rid of 'em.
Seelie	Don't you dare raise your voice in this house!
Danger	*(Courteously plausible)* Sure, I'm an oul' bum! No one takes any notice o' Danger Mullaly.
Kevin	*(Suddenly)* We'll have to be goin' or we'll miss the train.
Danger	I'll take the bags. *(He does so)*
Seelie	*(Exiting)* And don't come back! *(Exit Seelie)*
Kevin	*(To Peg – extending hand)* Goodbye! *(She accepts his hand half-heartedly)* I'll see you some time next year, please God! *(Kevin hurries out door, followed by Dinny)*
Peg	Good luck – Kevin!
Danger	*(Holdings bags – to Tom)* I often felt a strong an' wilful desire for the companionship of a woman, an' I was often plagued by the thought of what I was missin'. What I say is – thanks be to God that it isn't me that's sending them two sons away from their natural country, this fine summer's mornin'. *(Exits Danger)*
Tom	Danger is in a contrary mood this mornin'. And, look! he forgot his box of holy pictures.
Peg	He was tellin' the truth but he didn't tell it all. 'Tis stories about prostitutes an' easy money that carries half of 'em over there – that half doesn't be long comin' home again.
Tom	Not them two lads!
Peg	No – not them! You could see they were decent lads, especially the big fella – the way he put his hands around his brother. They're a pity, them two lads. No place to come home to, if they don't make out for themselves; no one wantin' them!
Tom	The big fella was on to you, Peg. Did you see him?
Peg	Every one is on to me! What else does a man do when he comes into a pub an' sees a girl workin' there? *(Thoughtfully)*

139

Although he wasn't like the rest of them … was he, Tom? You could see that about him. You could see he was a lad that was lookin' for nothin' soft; a lad that was out to make his own way in the world. *(Musingly)* He said he'd write to me! *(Laughs)* Sure, he'll have me forgotten the first Saturday night he lays eyes on a painted woman in the streets of London.

Tom He seemed a likely lad. Did you never think of goin' to London, Peg?

Peg I thought of it!

Tom You could take the baby, get a job maybe, an' do better for yourself than you're doin' here.

Peg I wouldn't give it to say to the sneakin' gossips o' Keelty that they put the wind up me.

Tom You know, I have a few thousand in my own name, and a few hundred fiddled in case I'd be stuck for money some time. I often thought about boltin' off an' leavin' her to herself … but she's my own an' there's no goin' for me.

Peg She's a good woman! Some one must have the reins. I don't want the money. Thanks all the same. *(Urgently)* What time is it?

Tom *(Looks out into bar)* Eleven – train time. *(Tom raises hand to command attention. In the distance the whistle of a train is heard)*

Peg *(Distantly)* I see the two of 'em sittin' down on their seats, an' their faces white an' the young fella cryin'. I can see their faces. I can see the train pullin' out o' the station. I can't help it, Tom. All them young boys an' girls, holdin' on tight to their bags, an' every minute feelin' their pockets in case their money was lost.

Tom *(A little hurt for her sake)* Don't be thinkin' too much about them things, Peg, for your own good.

(Peg whistles the first bars of Many Young Men of Twenty. *Then she sings it and in the distance [if that is feasible] a chorus of voices joins in)*

Peg/Voices Many young men of twenty said goodbye
It breaks my heart
To see the face of every girl and boy
It breaks my heart and now I'm fit to die
My boy Jimmy's gone from me
Sailed away across the sea

	My Jimmy's gone and here alone am I
	Many young men of twenty said goodbye.
Tom	I could almost hear the voices of the boys an' girls goin' away.
Peg	I feel the same thing every mornin' I hear that oul' train whistlin'.

(Tom clenches hand and lends an ear to the distance)

Tom   There's a quare voice comin' now!

Danger   *(Outside – singing)*

Ha-ha, says Mikey Houlihan, I'll tackle up my ass,
An' I'll put on my new brown suit, that I wears goin' to Mass
O, I'll put on my new brown suit, an' I'll put on my vest
I'll die for mother Ireland, the land that I love best.

(Enter Danger) Big crowd at the train this mornin'. I could have sold a dozen o' those only for forgettin' 'em. *(Looks severely at both Peg and Tom)* Ye know me well enough, the two of ye. Well, I'm goin' to do somethin' now that'll shock the sugar out of yeer shaggin' skins. *(Begins a search in obscure pockets of coat)* Excuse the language!

Peg   What way did the boys take it?

Danger   *(Half to himself, still fumbling about obscure pockets)* I have a reserve here some place.

Tom   Wouldn't you answer Peg, Danger, when she asks you a question?

Danger   Who? The two boys! Sure, God dammit, 'tis them that has me the way I am. The youngest one of 'em started cryin' before he went on the train. *(Pauses in his search)* An' what does Kevin do? He puts his hands on his head an' he says 'I love you, Dinny, an' I'll mind you!' an' he kissed him then. *(Pause)*

Peg   What else?

Danger   That was enough for Danger Mullaly! Sure, 'twould be the talk o' Keelty for two generations if I left a salt tear run down the side o' my face! *(Triumphantly)* Aaah! I have her! *(Produces ten shilling note and holds it on high)* I always keep this in reserve for fear of emergency. I told ye I was goin' to shock ye. *(Command)* Peg, bring us two large whiskeys an' keep the change! *(Peg looks at him anxiously)* An' be quick about it! *(Peg exits, taking ten shilling note)*

Tom   What notion possessed you to spend it?

Danger   'Twouldn't do your heart good to see them two young fellows goin'. I had to come away, man, I tell you. I couldn't be watchin' them cryin'. *(Plea)* Fair play to me now, Tom. If it got known within Keelty that Danger Mullaly stood a drink, I could never walk down the street again.

Tom   I won't say a word.

(Enter Peg with two whiskeys. Danger and Tom accept same)

Danger   Here's a safe journey to them two young lads. God go with them! *(Danger finishes his drink in a swallow, seizes his red box and prepares to exit)*

Tom   God go with them! … You're not going?

Danger   I am!

Tom   I never in my life before saw you standin' a drink to any man. The least I can do is to stand a one back.

Danger   *(At door – sadly)* If you ever see me inclined to stand a round of drinks again, notify the civic guards and tell them that Danger Mullaly wants to be certified.

(End of Act One)

Act Two

Scene One

Action takes place as before. The time is the late evening of a day one year later. Danger Mullaly sits in a half-drunken state and is bent over a table. On the table is a pint glass which is quarter filled with stout. Also on the table is his box of holy pictures. He addresses one of the pictures. Distant pipes or the sound of an oboe should introduce this soliloquy.

Danger   You gave me a lot o' rope, an' You're still givin' it to me. What good are fellows like Danger Mullaly to the world – useless, drunken oul' fools that everyone makes a joke of? What did I ever do for You? Every one in the village of Keelty condemns me, but You never condemned me, and I'm sellin' Your picture every day to fellows an' girls that throw it away ... No, that's not true ... They don't throw it away. You were never thrown away, but they forgot about You, or You're left in the bottom of a suitcase or You fall to the floor an' You're brushed out o' the room. But I'll keep on sellin' Your pictures *(Places his palms on the table and looks at picture thereon)* Great God, if I was there the day they crucified You, I'd beat what soldiers was at the foot of Calvary. *(Stands erect – corrects himself)* No! I wouldn't! I wouldn't! I'd go into some pub along the way an' meet a few fellows like myself or fellows like Kevin that went to England an' I'd say: 'Lads, lads, here's a great chance for us – our last chance ... They're bringin' Him up the road now an' they have a big Cross on His back an' 'tis knockin' Him.' I'd say then: 'We'll be cute now, lads. We'll get a few sticks an' a few stones an' we'll find a handy gable-end of a house an' we'll ambush 'em.' Then we'd wait, wait until the crowd that were followin' the procession were leapin' over us, to see the sight of Him an' He draggin' it after Him. An' I'd say then: 'Now, men, now!' an' I'd jump out in front of 'em, an' the first soldier I'd see I'd catch him by the throat an' I'd squeeze with all my strength, an' I'd say, very slow, 'Take that Cross off His back, you reptile!' An' then the crowd would rise up in anger against the soldiers an' you'd hear their curses a mile away, an' the day would be won … But no! He'd keep His Cross an' He'd say: 'Thanks, Danger! Thanks, oul' son! But this is the way!' an' he'd lift up His hand an' He'd say: 'Peace! Peace! Peace!'

(Danger finishes his pint and sings with feeling)

They crowned Your head with thorns, they brought You misery;
You died upon a Cross, high up in Calvary;
There is no other love for me;
You will be mine through all eternity.
Round here they laugh an' call me 'Drunken Danger!'
But I have you in spite of Keelty town;
The greatest pal that ever walked a roadway;
The only Man who never let me down.

(Enter Peg from bar, humming theme song)

That oul' song, again! They aren't all home yet from England, Peg. He might come!

Peg	He won't come! You know that, Danger!
Danger	You never know!
Peg	I heard every word you said there, when you were talkin' to yourself.
Danger	You did not!
Peg	I did! And, Danger, He won't be as hard on you as you think when you pass across. Sure, that's why He died, to be where the Judgement is, so that we'll all be treated fair.
Danger	I was drunk!
Peg	You were as sober as ever you'll be. Sure, aren't we all in the same boat. He'll allow for everything, Danger.
Danger	Everything?
Peg	I think He will! I think He'll make special allowance for you, seein' that you love Him so much.
Danger	*(Taking heart)* Do you know who's coming home tomorrow night?
Peg	There's always someone comin' home.
Danger	D'you remember the two young fellas who left for England that mornin' last year. You remember the tall, good-lookin' lad, surely, that stood me the pint. You remember him?
Peg	I remember the two boys an' their father an' mother.
Danger	That's right! Dawheen Timmineen Din, that was the father's name, a pauperised crab-jaw. I heard him boasting the other

144

	day in a pub how they were comin' back, his two sons. One of 'em is married.
Peg	Which one?
Danger	You needn't worry – it's the small lad.
Peg	As if I cared.
Danger	He was enquirin' what time the train came in.
Peg	Ten to seven.
Danger	I have to earn my few bob. Peg, bringin' down bags. I told him 'twas ten to eight.
	(Enter Tom from kitchen)
Tom	Give us a ball o' raw malt on the spot, Peg.
Peg	What about your sister?
Tom	Do as I say! I'm not goin' to stick this much longer. I can't even look sideways with her. Bring in that drink! *(Exit Peg. To Danger)* She says to me, before the tea: 'Show me a smell o' your breath!' I put my foot down and said 'My breath is my own!' She hit me a slap across the face.
Danger	'Tis bad to drink alone!
Tom	Now, now, now! I've enough problems!
Danger	I'll tell you about the civil war and where I was wounded during an ambush.
Tom	You wounded?
Danger	As bad as any of 'em; stabbed and stung and pierced …
Tom	By what?
Danger	Nettles! *(Enter Peg with a glass of whiskey. Tom accepts it)* Very few men can drink alone and find contentment.
Tom	You'll miss the train!
Danger	What time is it?
Tom	Train time!
Danger	*(Reluctantly goes to exit)* You won't stand?
Tom	I can't be standin' to you always.
Danger	I'd stand back if you did.
Tom	With what?
Danger	Out of this baby Paddy you hid in the turf shed. *(Exit Danger)*
Tom	Any evening paper?
Peg	I'll get it. *(Peg exits by door to bar. Tom sips whiskey cautiously. Enter Peg with paper. Tom accepts same and shrewdly conceals himself and whiskey behind paper)* I'm goin' in the back, to lock the store.

145

	(The paper nods. Exit Peg)
Tom	*(Reads aloud)* 'Ballinacourtney Bridge Congress declared open' … *(Mutters)* … 'What's Wrong with Irish Jumpers? … is it ganseys they mean, now, or horses? … 'CIE Buffet burned over closing of West Cork Railway' … 'Ass an' car abandoned in Bandon' … *(Enter a well-dressed man of thirty. Tom suddenly discards paper and furiously seeks to conceal whiskey. The entrant is Maurice Brown)*
Maurice	It's all right, Tom! It's only me!
Tom	Good God, man, you frightened the wits outa me! I thought 'twas Seelie. *(Maurice sits wearily aside)*
Tom	Well? How do you like Keelty?
Maurice	Too early to judge.
Tom	How do you like your digs?
Maurice	Tom, all digs are mediocre! If they were good they'd be hotels. All hotels are mediocre. If they were good they wouldn't be open to the public.
Tom	Will you join me in a drop of this?
Maurice	I'll chance it. *(Tom rises)*
Tom	Do you like the school?
Maurice	All schools are the same, Tom – the same smell, the same sadness, the same teachers. Get them through the course but teach them nothing. That's all you have to do, Tom. I teach English. *(Bitterly)* Do you know what I teach, Tom – twenty prescribed poems and ten prescribed essays and one prescribed play. I've taught in four different schools by prescription only. This is the age of the specialist.
Tom	I'll bring in the drink.
	(Exit Tom. Maurice rises and looks into the fireplace)
Maurice	*(To fireplace)* Withered broom and roses with cankerous appendages. *(Turns and shouts to Tom)* Who is this Peg Finnerty, Tom?
Tom	*(Shouts from bar)* One minute and I'll be in to you with the drinks.
Maurice	*(Shouts back)* Why I ask is because most of the young lads at the school come into the bar here on their way home from school and I know they're not coming to see you. *(Enter Tom with two glasses of whiskey. He hands one to Maurice)* Am I to understand you're buying?

Tom   You can buy the next one if Seelie doesn't come in. *(They both sit)*

Maurice   About Peg Finnerty?

Tom   If Seelie comes in, you can let on you insisted on I having a drink. You're well-spoken and educated.

Maurice   Tom, when I came home a week ago to teach in a school, yours was the first bar I entered. You were in the same predicament then. Being a stranger in the locality I suggested, improperly perhaps, that the barman have a drink with me. You readily acquiesced. We exchanged confidences Tom. You told me about Seelie and I told you about the reason for my being dismissed from my last school and the school before that and the school before that, Tom. We became confidants. Now I have asked you a question and for some unknown reason, you baulk me. *(At the end of his tether)* Who is Peg Finnerty, Tom? And, Tom, I didn't come here to listen to your troubles. I have enough of my own.

Tom   Good luck! *(They quaff)* As you know, she works here with me. She's only just gone out now to lock the store and she should be in.

Maurice   Go on, Tom!

Tom   Her history you want, isn't it?

Maurice   If I want to know why ten candidates for the Leaving Certificate stop at your bar, three out of six evenings, the answer is yes!

Tom   *(Comfortable)* She comes from a small farm a few miles from here. She used be doin' a line with a schoolmaster's son. He used play with the county team – maybe you heard of him – Jimmy Farrelly?

Maurice   Never heard of him! Go on, Tom!

Tom   I'll put it in brief for you. She was in receipt of a child from him and he buzzed off like a wasp. *(Whiskeys are supped)*

Maurice   All wasps fly after they sting. But why do my young English pupils stop off here on their way home?

Tom   Songs, Maurice! Songs! She's a great hand to sing songs and she can make them up as she goes along.

Maurice   A rare quality! I'll have to hear her some time.

Tom   Do me a favour! When she comes in now, ask her to sing the song she made up about Kitty Curley.

Maurice	Who the hell is Kitty Curley?
Tom	Another one of the clients that come in here. You didn't meet her yet?
Maurice	Not yet! What's she like?
Tom	Oh, she has a shawl and she's oldish now, but she used be a great favourite when the British army was here. She tells fortunes. The same oul' scrawl – you'll meet a black man on your travels. Beware of a woman called MOC … and that you'll cross water … you know, that sort of stuff … Don't say a word now, she's coming in. I'll introduce you nice and proper to her and you can form your own opinion, provided you ask her to sing.
Maurice	Don't worry. I'll ask her. I like a song.
	(Peg is heard singing)
Peg	*(Singing)* The dawn is breaking now, where fields are wet with dew
	And in my lonely heart are memories of you
	(Closing door behind her)
	There is no other love for me
	You will be mine through all eternity.
	(Peg sees Maurice and stops suddenly)
Maurice	Please, go on!
	(Peg looks at him for a moment and then goes on, looking at him in a hardboiled way)
Peg	*(Singing)* You will be mine while stars of night are shining
	And we shall sleep until we meet again;
	The stars have fled and shades of night are pining;
	The dawn won't break, my love, until we meet again.
Maurice	He must have been a considerate lover!
Peg	Who?
Maurice	Jimmy Farrelly! *(Points at Tom immediately)* He told me.
Tom	I told him, Peg, how you could sing and a few more things. Peg, this is Maurice Browne. He's a secondary teacher after coming to town here. I was tellin' you about him. This is Peg Finnerty, Maurice. *(They exchange 'How do you do's')*
Maurice	I've heard a lot about your singing.
Peg	Really?
Maurice	The lads at the school never stop talking about you.
Peg	There's more than the lads at school talkin' about me!

Tom	It's a small town.
Maurice	How about a song now?
Peg	Sorry! I'm not in the mood.
Maurice	That's a pity. I heard you were good.
Peg	Oh, you did, did you? And what else did you hear … ?
Maurice	Nothing! Why?
Peg	You're all the same, aren't you? *(To Tom)* You're just as bad!
Maurice	I didn't mean to offend! *(Tom exits to bar)* Do you make up these songs yourself, or what?
Peg	Well, if you want to know … I do!
Maurice	Strange!
Peg	Is it? I'm educated, if that's what you mean. I spent a few years with the nuns and learned how to play the piano but, of course, because I'm a servant girl, it's strange. That's what makes it strange, isn't it, my being a servant girl?
Maurice	Well, why don't you leave? You could get a job in England.
Peg	And leave my baby?
Maurice	Oh!
Peg	*(Mimics)* Oh!
Maurice	Well, what's wrong with being a servant girl?
Peg	Don't make me laugh! How much a week do you earn?
Maurice	Well, with tax deducted, about £12.
Peg	Do you know how much I earn? Thirty bob a week. And do you know how long I work? From 8 in the morning till 8 at night, 12 hours a day with every second Sunday off and a half-day every week. Of course I'm the luckiest servant girl alive in Keelty because I work with Tom Hannigan who is the best-off man in the town, but the other girls are shoved into work when they're fifteen. They're not human beings – they're beasts of burden. Do they get an hour for lunch? What a hope! Of course, to hear the ladies of fashion in Keelty talking, you'd swear they were doing the girls a favour. *(Apes a Keelty lady of fashion)* 'I have to train her, you know! Couldn't let her near the cooker. Off to dances every chance she gets and jaded in the mornings.' *(Reverts to herself)* And then when she's trained, what does she get? Periodic raises until she has enough to dress like a decent girl. No bloody fear! If she goes to England, she's supposed to be ungrateful, or they'll say: 'Oh! she'll get her senses there!' *(Viciously)* Oh, to every little servant-girl, I say:

149

'Clear to hell out of it – to England where you'll be treated like a human being, where the boys of your own class earn as much as the schoolteachers here, and where you'll have a chance of marrying and dressing decently and where, when you go into a dance hall, you'll meet nice boys, not like the farmers' and the shopkeepers' sons and the university students of Ireland who want nothing from you but a good night of pleasure and who'd be ashamed of their sacred lives to talk to you in the street the day after.'

Maurice   You're very hard-boiled!

Peg   I was cooked all right!

Maurice   Don't pick me up wrong now, but would you mind if I took you out some night?

Peg   Oh, I won't pick you up wrong! I know exactly what you mean. You have a car, naturally! We'll go to the pictures in Cork City some night. Early house. A few drinks after. And home then. But what a homecoming!

Maurice   That's what I had in mind, but not the way you think. *(Seriously)* We'd go to the pictures here in Keelty if you like and I'd be honoured if you did no more than walk down the street with me.

Peg   I didn't mean to be so hard. Thanks for the offer.

Maurice   You'll come so?

Peg   No, I won't! Sorry!
(Enter Danger)

Danger   A half-one, quick, Peg! *(Exit Peg. Danger sizes up Maurice, shakes his head and winks at him tentatively)* Very weathery! *(Silence)* A draft o' low pressure on the wireless.
(Enter Peg. Hands whiskey to Danger)

Maurice   Put that down to me, Peg!

Peg   How's it going, Danger?

Danger   Three bags for Moran's Hotel. Yanks. *(Exit Peg)* Who's that you are?

Maurice   Maurice Browne. I'm the new teacher.

Danger   I remember the fellow that was here before you. Pioneer! Never smoked! A terrible man for talking Irish. Good luck! *(Drinks his whiskey)* If I score well out of these fellows, I'll stand back to you. The fellow before you used teach history. Always talkin' about Brian Boru and Finnbarr MacCool. Do you teach

	history, too?
Maurice	I try to!
Danger	D'you see the hotel I'm goin' to now? There's a great short history of Ireland there.
Maurice	*(Interested)* Is there?
Danger	All wrote down by an ordinary painter on the front door.
Maurice	*(Puzzled)* What is it?
Danger	A short history of modern Ireland – in one word – Pull!
	(Exit Danger)

CURTAIN

Act Two

Scene Two

Action takes place as before. The time is train time (due in) of the following evening. Peg Finnerty is sweeping kitchen. Then she sits at table dejectedly, and commences to sing.

Peg	I'll be waiting for you where the cockerel cries,
	Down here in Keelty where the heart in me dies;
	I'll be waiting for you till the heart in me sighs
	For the strength and love of you down here in Keelty.
	(Unnoticed, Maurice Browne enters and listens, unobserved Peg continues to sing)
	I'll be waiting for you where the small waters flow
	Down here in Keelty where the whitethorns grow
	The white fires of joy in your bosom will glow
	When you see your fine babe in my arms down here in Keelty.
	(After a moment, Maurice Browne claps and Peg turns, surprised, to see him) You shouldn't do that!
Maurice	What?
Peg	Sneak up on a person.
Maurice	I asked you to sing several times and you refused. I availed of an opportunity.
Peg	*(Rises and commences to brush)* I like courtesy in people. You might have coughed. I wouldn't mind singing. I felt like singing and I sang but I don't like it when a man spies on a woman.
Maurice	Unless the woman wants him to spy!
Peg	You must have known a lot of women?
Maurice	A few!
Peg	In that case you're wasting your time with me.
Maurice	Don't misunderstand me. I'm just a human being.
Peg	Oh, this human being baloney! I was a human being too, but I'm not any more.
Maurice	I just want to take you out for a night.
Peg	Why don't you be completely honest and tell me what happens if I do?

Maurice	That's up to you.
Peg	That's the standard answer.
Maurice	I want to take you to a picture in Cork because there are hotels there. When the picture finishes, I would appreciate if you had several drinks with me, and you can do what you like then.
Peg	After several drinks! Do what I like?
Maurice	Yes! *(Peg laughs)*
Peg	But I never took several drinks in my life.
Maurice	We'll have a few drinks, then. One or two.
Peg	And if the night doesn't work out for you, you'll never talk to me again. Isn't that it?
Maurice	No! – that's not true.
Peg	You're honest, Maurice, only when I prompt you. The rest of the honesty you leave up to me.
Maurice	No! No! That's not true, Peg.
Peg	Look, Maurice! I've been honest with you. If you said to me: 'Come to bed with me!' I'd be honoured but I'd say 'No!' If you said 'marry me!' I'd be honoured but I'd also say 'No!' Now listen carefully to me, Maurice. If you said: 'Come out and get plastered drunk with me because I'm lost to the world and I have friends nowhere and I'll probably get sick when I go to bed' I would probably go with you because I'd feel sorry for you and I'd think it was my fault and you'd need me.
Maurice	You're a very wise old woman!
Peg	A servant girl has to be wise. One slip and all is lost.
	(Enter Danger burdened with suitcases which he proceeds to deposit in a convenient corner)
Danger	They're back! *(Enter Kevin looking much the same as when he went. Peg shakes hands with him and welcomes him home and introduces him to Maurice)*
Maurice	I have to be going. See you later, Peg. *(Exit Maurice)*
Danger	I'd better give your brother a hand with the rest of the bags.
Peg	Your brother married?
Kevin	Oh! – you heard?
Peg	Danger heard your father talking in a pub.
Kevin	I'm surprised my father wasn't there to meet us.
Peg	Danger gave him the wrong time for the train … Why didn't you marry, too?

Kevin	Plenty time for that!
Peg	I suppose you know it all now – after a year in London?
Kevin	No more than I did when I left. I worked hard.
Peg	Do you like your job?
Kevin	I do. I'm a charge-hand now.
Peg	Good!
Kevin	Did you go dancing since I left?
Peg	No! Did you?
Kevin	No.
Peg	Sit down now, Kevin. Your brother wasn't long finding himself a wife.
Kevin	He was lonely and she was lonely. It isn't so bad over there when you have some one to go home to at night.
Peg	I suppose you'll be the next to marry?
Kevin	Maybe! You never answered my letters.
Peg	I know. I'm sorry about that.
	(Enter Danger with additional suitcases which he deposits followed by Dinny and Dinny's wife. Dinny is dressed elegantly, hair slicked, narrow trousers, etc. His wife is young, frail and wears tight-fitting red trousers, tight-fitting yellow sweater and hair in a pony-tail. Dinny with a marked Cockney accent introduces his wife – Dot – to Peg)
Danger	Here they are an' wait till you see what he's after landin' home from London.
Dinny	Peg, this is Dot. Dot, this is Peg.
Peg	How do you do?
Dinny	Put it down over there, darling!
	(Dot sits at table, R.)
Kevin	How about a drink?
Dot	Gin and lime!
Dinny	Scotch!
Danger	A pint!
Kevin	And I'll have a pint.
Peg	*(Repeats)* Gin and lime, Scotch and two pints. *(Exit Peg)*
Danger	Sit down, let ye. *(They sit. Enter Tom)*
Tom	Is Peg lookin' after ye?
Kevin	She is, Tom.
	(Tom welcomes them home and is introduced to Dot)
Tom	Well, how do you like Ireland?

Dot	I 'aven't seen much of it yet, 'ave I? The sausages got a nice flavour.
Tom	Eh?
Dot	The sausages – they got a nice flavour.
Tom	*(Confused)* I'll give Peg a hand in the bar. *(Exit Tom)*
Danger	I expect yeer father will be here shortly. He'll be greatly surprised to meet *(to Dinny)* your Missus.
Dinny	He'll get used to it.
Danger	There's a big change in you from the day you left. You were stinkin' cryin' that mornin'!
Dinny	Wot?
Kevin	It was the same at every station along the way, Danger. 'Twould make anybody cry. Young boys and girls leaving home for the first time. Fathers and mothers heartbroken, turnin' their heads away to hide the tears. 'Twould turn you against railway stations.
	(Enter Peg bearing tray of drinks which she distributes. Kevin pays her. She leaves)
Danger	Here's to Dáil Éireann and the Irish language!
	(He quaffs. They all quaff. Dinny gulps his back)
Dot	Wot's Dáil Éireann?
Danger	Dáil Éireann? The only place in Ireland where the civil war is still going on!
	(Enter Peg with Kevin's change)
Dinny	*(To Peg – handing her his glass)* Fill that again and make it a double this time.
Kevin	You'll be drunk.
Dinny	I want plenty of ammunition before I meet the old man. *(Exit Peg with glass. She returns with glass of whiskey. Dinny snatches it and swallows it. He hands Peg money. Enter Kitty Curley followed by a man wearing a melodeon strapped about his shoulders. He has a shade over one eye and a hat far too large for him. Kitty goes straight to the English girl and takes her hand. Kitty wears a shawl about her shoulders, is fiftyish, grey and wears wellingtons)*
Kitty	Tell your fortune, Miss?
	(Danger intercepts Kitty's hand)
Danger	Tell my fortune, Kitty darling.
Kitty	*(Looks at his hand)* You'll pass water before the night is out – the way your drinkin' porter.

	(Danger, holding her hand, kneels and commences to sing while others clap their hands)

Danger When I land in dear Dáil Éireann
Kitty I will marry you!
An ermine coat you will be wearin'
The TDs' wives will all be rearin'
I love pretty Kitty Curley,
'Deed I do! 'Deed I do!
(Danger rises and dances about Kitty while the melodeon player plays a bar. Peg comes upstage to sing)

Peg I love pretty Kitty Curley, 'deed I do! 'deed I do!
Love her late, I love her early.
Love her 'cause her teeth are pearly
I love pretty Kitty Curley, 'deed I do, 'deed I do.
(All join in while Danger still executes dance)

All I love pretty Kitty Curley, 'deed I do! 'deed I do!
Love her late, I love her early
Love her 'cause her teeth are pearly
I love pretty Kitty Curley, 'deed I do, 'deed I do!
(Exit Peg. Dinny calls Tom from the bar while Kevin exchanges conversation. Enter Tom. Dinny indicates crowd and Tom exits to bar)

Danger What about a song from the little Englishwoman? *(All vent approval)*

Dinny *(Proudly)* She used to sing in a shebeen over!

Dot It wasn't a shebeen. It was a night club. They called it a night club anyway.

Danger Come on and give us the song!

Dot *(Singing in a tinny Cockney voice)*
Let X be equal to my love for you
It's as simple as ABC
Because I'm a mathematician in the very best tradition
So let X be equal to my love for you.
Let Y be equal to your love for me
It's as simple as ABC
Put the X and the Y together and we'll soon discover whether
We will mingle mathematically.
Take the square root of love and divide by the stars above
Take one quarter of a moon and a sweet romantic tune
Take a circle from a ring you're sure to see mathematically.

Let Y be equal to your love for me
It's as simple as ABC
Put the X and the Y together and we'll soon discover whether
We will mingle mathematically
It's as simple as ABC.
(All applaud politely)

Danger   Imagine learning that in Irish? *(Enter Peg with the drinks, followed by Tom who has a glass of whiskey for Kitty Curley and the melodeon player, Dinny pays Peg. Peg exits with money)* You should hear Peg singing! *(To melodeon player)* A waltz! The one Peg sings! *(Melodeon player starts to play the waltz 'I am a Servant Girl'. Danger bows elaborately and asks Kitty Curley to dance. They lead the floor. Dinny and Dot follow them. Peg enters and Kevin waltzes with her. After a moment of waltzing Peg takes Kevin's hand and stands facing audience. She sings while the others dance in the background)*

Peg   *(Singing)* I am a servant girl, fair game to one and all
At thirty bob a week, I am the beck and call
The Golf Club won't have me as you can plainly see
I am a servant girl, the Miss in Misery.
(Peg waltzes around again to the music and stops after a circuit)
All this is very fine, the drinking and the song;
It happens all the time, why must it happen wrong?
How simple now for you to say that you'll be true?
How simple now for me to whisper – I love you!
(They waltz around again and the music suddenly stops. Tom disappears into bar and everybody is stock still under Miss Seelie's icy glare)

Seelie   *(Calls loudly)* Tom! … Tom! … *(Dejectedly Tom returns)* What's going on here? I just go down the street to the chapel and I find the scruff of the village here when I come back!

Kitty   Tell your fortune, Miss Seelie. *(She suddenly takes Seelie's hand)*

Seelie   *(Withdraws her hand in distaste. To Tom)* I'll be back in five minutes and I want to see him gone! *(Points to Danger)* and her *(Points to Kitty)* and him *(Points to melodeon player)* gone!
(Exits Seelie)

Danger   'Tis oul' gazebos like her that has this country the way it is! There's hundreds of young wans wantin' to get married an' there's her an' her likes addlin' the priests. Sure the priests have no time for her! 'Tis oul' sinners like me the priests want.

	(*To Kitty*) Bring on the melodeon player. I see a crowd of Yanks gettin' off the train. They'll be in the bar at Moran's Hotel now.
Kitty	I'll tell fortunes and you can sell holy pictures.
Danger	'Tenshun!
	(*Melodeon player, Kitty and Danger spring to attention and to the strains of 'Kitty Curley' exit*)
Peg	(*To Dot*) Are you long married?
Dinny	(*Slips hand around Dot's waist*) Nearly a week!
Dot	It seems like yesterday! I found him on the street one night an' 'e couldn't find 'is way 'ome. I been takin' 'im 'ome ever since.
Dinny	I'd be lost only for her.
	(*Enter Danger in a furious hurry*)
Danger	They're comin'! They're comin'!
All	Who?
Danger	(*Points at Kevin and Dinny*) Their father an' mother, Dawheen Timmineen Din and his missus. I wouldn't miss it for the world. (*Dot whispers into Dinny's ear. Dinny in turn whispers into Danger's ear. Danger takes Dot by the arm and leads her to door which he opens. He points expansively*) Up to the end of the yard an' you'll see a field an' it's the first furze bush you see after that. (*Exit Dot. To Kevin, indicating Peg*) She was all the time talkin' about you while you was away.
Peg	I was not, indeed! I had something else to be doin'.
Danger	(*To Kevin*) When are you goin' back?
Kevin	A week's time.
Danger	You'll nearly be married the next time you come.
Kevin	Maybe. (*Peg looks at him in some alarm. Enter Dawheen Timmineen Din, followed by his wife Maynan*)
DTD	(*To Danger*) You're the lyin' impostor that told me the train wouldn't be in till eight o'clock.
	(*Maynan meanwhile shakes hands with Kevin and Dinny*)
Danger	(*Dignity*) I never said anything of the kind!
DTD	Liar! I've a mind to give you a lash of this whip!
	(*Danger squares out, safely away from him, assumes a boxer's posture and does some fancy footwork. Dawheen ignores him and shakes hands with Kevin and Dinny*)
DTD	(*To Dinny*) Where's the wife?
Dinny:	She's out in the back. She'll be in shortly.

DTD	Is she a Catholic?
Dinny	I don't know what she is, but she's a lovely singer.
DTD	Had she a fortune?
Dinny	Oh, she had!
DTD	How much?
Dinny	Thirty bob.
DTD	What?
Dinny	That's a big fortune in England. *(Enter Dot. DTD and Maynan look appalled)* This is her! Dot, this is my father and mother, Dad, this is Dot! *(DTD is too surprised to say anything)*
Dot	*(Breezily)* Hello, Dad! *(Impulsively pecks Maynan on the cheek)* When do we go?
Dinny	We'll have a drink first.
DTD	No … No drink! *(Turns to Danger)* I'm like a braddy cow above around the railway station all over him.
Danger	Dawheen Timmineen Din, with his hands out for money. The more he has the more he wants.
Dinny	I must give you a present of a few pounds, Dad. *(Dinny impulsively takes wallet from his pocket and extracts several pounds. DTD advances eagerly to accept them but Dot snatches them and tucks them inside her sweater)*
Dot	Silly clot! Wot's 'e want it for? … *(Takes DTD by the hand)* Come on, Dad … let's hit for the old mud cabin! *(Danger and Dinny take the bags between them and exit together with DTD, Maynan and Dot singing 'It's as Simple as ABC.' Kevin stands abashed for a while. Peg begins to collect empty glasses)*
Kevin	Can I take you out walking tomorrow night?
Peg	Walking?
Kevin	Well, the weather is fine and the evenings are long. We could go by the river where the swans are.
Peg	Sorry! I never go out on dates with boys now.
Kevin	I think that's foolish. You're young and it's the summer time and why should you shut yourself away. You've every right to go walking – better right than anybody in Keelty because you're prettier than anybody here.
Peg	It takes courage! I've left it go so long now that I can't face it.
Kevin	I used always walk where the swans were before I went away. 'Twould be a thousand miles nicer if you were with me.
Peg	Can't you get some girl who hadn't my trouble? You'll get

	plenty here to go with you.
Kevin	You're the only girl I want with me. It would only be lonelier with any other girl.
Peg	I don't know! I wish you wouldn't be so nice about it. It makes it harder for me to have to say no.
Kevin	Just this once!
Peg	But what would people say?
Kevin	Well, if they're talking about us, they can't be talkin' about anybody else.
Peg	You're too persistent for me, but you don't understand. *(Enter Danger)*
Danger	*(To Kevin)* Your man is havin' canaries outside. You'd better come on. *(Exit Danger)*
Kevin	Right! I'm comin'! *(Looks at Peg)* I wouldn't ask you if I didn't mean it – there's no harm in my heart. *(Kevin looks dejectedly at Peg, Kevin exits. After a moment's hesitation Peg goes to door)*
Peg	*(Calls out)* Don't forget the swans … sometime … *(She closes the door quickly and leans with back to it and sings the first verse of 'Keelty')*

(END OF ACT TWO)

Action takes place as before. The time is the morning of one week later. In the back room Maurice Browne sits with a drink. Enter Peg from the bar.

Peg I had no idea you were goin' by train this mornin'.

Maurice *(Sullen)* Well the school is closed for holidays. You hardly expect me to spend them here.

Peg Where will you go? Home?

Maurice No, I won't go home. I don't know, Peg; I don't know what I'll do.

(Enter a heavily built middle-aged man with a youth of eighteen. They are father and son. The father is J. J. Houlihan, a local TD. The son is Johnny Houlihan. The father wears a hat of the Homburg variety)

Peg *(Respectfully)* Good morning, J.J. – Johnny.

J.J. Ah, Peg, how are you? And how's that young garsún o' yours?

Peg Fine, J.J.! Fine!

J.J. You've great guts, Peg. Great guts! And who's this man here? Do I know him?

Peg Hardly, J.J. This is Maurice Browne, the new secondary teacher. Maurice, this is J. J. Houlihan, the TD. and his son Johnny. *(Nods of acceptance are exchanged)*

Maurice Houlihan … ! *(Thoughtfully)* Are you anything to Mikey Houlihan that Danger Mullaly sings about?

J.J. *(Proudly)* Only his nephew! You know all about Mikey Houlihan, my uncle? One second … Peg, give us a drink. Whiskey for you, I see. A large whiskey for Mr Browne, Peg, an orange for Johnny and – what will I have? *(Explains to Maurice)* … I had a hard night last night – give me a drop of brandy, Peg.

Peg Right, Sir! *(Exit Peg)*

J.J. Sit down, Johnny. *(Both J.J. and Johnny sit. To Maurice)* Mikey Houlihan's name is respected far and wide.

Maurice *(Finishing his drink)* I have a curious nature, Mr Houlihan. Forgive me! You probably won't buy me any more whiskeys, but

	– how did your uncle die?
J.J.	Shot by an English officer. He was a marked man. They were out for his blood. *(Confidential)* There was more than that to it, too.
Maurice	The way I understand it from Danger Mullaly, he was shot by accident.
J.J.	*(Plausibly)* Don't mind that bum!
Maurice	*(Accepting drink from Peg, who has entered)* Danger Mullaly says he was shot by accident while he was carrying a gallon of water home to his grandmother.

(J.J. and Johnny accept their drinks from Peg. J.J. hands her a pound note)

J.J.	Keep the change out of that, Peg and buy a pair of nylons for yourself. *(Exit Peg. Still plausible)* If I had time I'd explain to you fully about my uncle's history but my son and I are catching the train.
Maurice	*(Finishing his drink)* So am I!
J.J.	*(Proudly)* Johnny here is starting off on his new job today in the north of the county.
Maurice	What job?
J.J.	Rate collector.
Maurice	I take it, he has the qualifications?
J.J.	Oh?
Maurice	Leaving certificate or clerical experience; experience and trustworthiness in the handling of money.
J.J.	*(Dangerous)* I bought you a drink because you were here alone. That doesn't mean you can insult me and get away with it.
Maurice	*(Calls)* Peg! The same again! *(Maurice finishes his drink. So does Johnny. So does J.J. after consideration. Enter Peg. She collects their glasses and exits. Rises and stands well apart from J.J.)* Tell me Mr Houlihan, how many other candidates were there for the job your son has?
J.J.	You have a job in this town, sonny boy. Mind it!
Johnny	Six – three of them were lads with their Leaving and the other three were clerks in the County Council offices.
J.J.	*(Ferociously – to son)* Shut up!
Maurice	And yet you get the job, and I take it you never went near a secondary school.

Johnny	Useless at books, but I can paint gorgeous pictures o' race-horses. *(Enter Peg with drinks. Maurice pays her with a pound note)*
Maurice	*(To Peg)* Keep the change out of that and stick it on to your Leaving Certificate. *(Exit Peg. She returns partly to door leading in from the bar)*
J.J.	See here, son – you'd better watch out!
Maurice	Don't threaten me, you smug, ignorant cabóg! What about the other lads who were all better qualified than your son?
J.J.	You won't have any job here when you get back. I guarantee you that! *(Enter Danger Mullaly. He is dressed respectably in a suit far too large for him. He carries a brown-papered parcel in his hand)*
Danger	Good mornin', Maurice! Is that the great J.J. Houlihan himself I see? How'll they manage in the Dáil without you at all?
J.J.	What are you all dressed up for today?
Danger	I'm being received at Arus an Uachtaráin by the chief. I hear they're building a monument to Mikey Houlihan, your uncle?
J.J.	That's right! The Taoiseach himself will be down for the un-veiling.
Danger	*(Sings)* God be with you, Mikey Houlihan, the pride of Keelty town An anointed bloody idiot, and a born bloody clown. You never fired a rifle, and you never heard a drum You died for dear old Ireland with a bullet in your bum.
J.J.	*(Jumps to his feet with fists clenched)* Take that back! Take it back! By Jingoes, I didn't take that from the Tans not to mind you! *(Danger retreats behind Maurice's back and raises his fists when he is safe)*
Danger	Twenty-two years in Dáil Éireann and never opened his mouth, except to pick his teeth!
Maurice	*(To J.J.)* Simmer down!
J.J.	A bloody turncoat, that's what! I never changed my politics.
Maurice	And you never will. You have the same politics as your father before you, and your sons after you will have the same politics. That's this damn country all over. You're all blinded by the past. You're still fighting the civil war. Well, we don't give a tinker's curse about the civil war or your damn politics, or the past. The future we have to think about. If there was any

	honest politician, he'd be damned. If Our Lord walked down the main street of Keelty tomorrow morning, ye'd crucify him again. We're sick to death of hypocrisy and the glories of the past. Keep the Irish language and find jobs for the lads that have to go to England. Forget about the six counties and straighten out the twenty-six first.
Danger	I'd give 'em six more if I had my way.
J.J.	*(Furious – to son)* You wait here! I'm not travellin' on a train with this bloody crew. I'll get a car and we'll drive up.
Danger	Up Connolly!
J.J.	Communists, that's what ye are! Bloody Communists! *(J.J. exits. Danger glowers at Johnny)*
Johnny	Don't want that job at all! The man that should have got it is a married man with two kids. I've my fare for England and that's where I'm going.
Danger	Good bloody man you are!
Johnny	Would you meet any Cork men in London?
Danger	Oh, you would! Stop in the middle of London one night and shout 'Echo!' and everyone that turns his head will be a Cork man.
Peg	*(To Danger)* Did I hear you say you were goin' to England?
Danger	That's right!
Peg	But how … why?
Danger	Because I'm lonesome, that's why, an' because I have pride, too. Your man Kevin gave me the fare an' he's gettin' a job for me, too. I'll be treated fair there anyway.
Peg	I can hardly believe it. What's in the parcel?
Danger	*(Retrieves parcel)* A couple of pounds of Drisheen for the Dook! *(Enter Kitty Curley followed by melodeon player)*
Kitty	Ah, Danger, me darlin', I heard it below in Moran's Hotel. You're off across the water. Didn't I always read it in your fortune. Show here! *(Takes his hand)* You'll marry an elderly widow-woman with money in the post office and a poodle dog. Ye'll have no family but ye'll adopt a black baby and he'll be the first black TD in Dáil Éireann. *(She sees Johnny)* Tell your fortune for a bob! *(She takes Johnny's hand)* You'll marry a woman with blond hair on her head and black hair under her oxter. You'll be Lord Mayor of Dagenham and you'll be chased by a Poll-Angus bull.

Johnny	Japers tell me no more! That's my father! Here's your money.
Danger	Bring us one last drink for the road, Peg. Bring me a ball o' raw malt. Bring us all malt. *(Exit Peg. To Kitty)* I'll send you a pair of false teeth from England, Kitty.
Kitty	I'll keep the ones I have. I'm not in the habit of dismissin' faithful servants. They were white an' pearly one time an' there's many a gay soldier could tell you the same. Give us one ould song, Danger, before you go!
Danger	*(Singing)* I'd sooner join the Foreign Legion What in hell am I to do? I've no wife or son or daughter, I've a chance across the water I love pretty Kitty Curley, 'deed I do, 'deed I do! *(Peg enters with tray of drinks)*
Danger	Come on! All together!
All	*(Singing)* I love pretty Kitty Curley, 'deed I do, 'deed I do Love her late, I love her early Love her 'cause her teeth are pearly I love pretty Kitty Curley, 'deed I do, 'deed I do!
Kitty	*(Singing)* Cross my palm or you're a goner I know what life holds for you I tells fortunes for a tanner Tells the truth, upon my honour. All the lads know Kitty Curley 'Deed they do! 'Deed they do! *(All repeat chorus. Peg distributes the drinks and collects money from Danger)*
Danger	Ladies and gentlemen, a toast! To the Emigration Commission! *(They quaff)* To the new Licensing Laws! They'll tell us what time to go to bed next. *(They quaff)*
Kitty	To the West Cork Railway! *(They quaff)*
Maurice	To Danger Mullaly, the Navigator! *(They cheer this)* Speech! Suas ar an ardan. *(They hoist Danger on to a table)*
Danger	*(Gutturally)* A Chairde Ghael! O, Uh, Gu, Bo, Boola, Bo, Wo Bow Wow! I always believe in a few words in Irish first. *(Applause)* Men an' women o' Keelty, there's tears in my eyes an' an ache in my heart to be leavin' the country o' my birth this grand summer's mornin'. But I go proudly because I know that the TDs and the ministers above in Dáil Éireann will be

cryin' their eyes out after I'm gone, an' the Holy Josies will be prayin' for me so that I won't stray from the path. I'll be a member of the IBNA next week an' forever more I'll be disgraced in the eyes of my schoolmasters who taught me for better things.

Kitty   What's the IBNA Danger?

Danger   The Irish Buck Navvies Association! (*Quotes poem*)
When I was a young man my books I attended
But a poor man's a poor man, I know to my grief
So I'll be a buck navvy, as God has intended
And work with my hands for the cheat and the thief.
(*Cheers from listeners*)
We can't all be doctors, we can't all be teachers.
To England I'll go, where there's money in sweat
So here's a farewell to the religious preachers
From an Irish buck navvy who goes to his death.
(*Cheers from listeners*)
Oh, young men of twenty, I issue fair warning,
There's no hope for me since I failed at my books;
Stay here in old Ireland this fine summer's morning,
And save her from politics, chancers and crooks.
(*Cheers from listeners*)
The wild geese are gone, but the goslings are flying;
The young men of twenty are leaving the land.
The old men are old, and the old men are dying.
Stay here in old Ireland and make a last stand.
(*Cheers from listeners*)
Take me down off this shaggin' table an' let me finish my drink.
(*They help him from table*)

Kitty   Peg, give us one touch o' that oul' song o' yours!

Peg   'Tis too early in the mornin' for singin'!

Maurice   For me, Peg?

Peg   (*Humorously*) For you, Maurice. (*In her hard-boiled way*) Anything for you, Maurice!

Kitty   D' you know the song you'll sing, me bonny barmaid? Sing that song about goin' away. Fool I was I didn't go when I was young an' handsome – I might have a husband now and be naggin' the nose off his face.

Danger   Put her up on the table, the same as me. Peg is a coulogeous

	singer. *(Peg is lifted up on the table)*
Kitty	Give us our own song.
	(Approval is evident from the others on stage)
Peg	*(Sings)* Many young men of twenty said goodbye
	I had a son,
	A healthy love-child and a bonny boy
	Many young men of twenty said goodbye
	My boy Jimmy went away
	Maurice Browne is here, to stay
	Maurice Browne is here, and here am I –
	Many young men of twenty said goodbye.
	(All join in the chorus)
All	Many young men of twenty said goodbye
	All that long day
	From break of dawn until the sun was high
	Many young men of twenty said goodbye
	My boy Jimmy went that day
	On the big ship sailed away
	Sailed away and left me here to die
	Many young men of twenty said goodbye.
	(Peg is lifted from the table)
Danger	*(Toasts)* To Elizabeth the Second of England and to the jobs she has waitin' for me! *(Enter Kevin carrying suitcase. Danger immediately shakes his hand)* Where's the rest of 'em?
Kevin	They're on their way – I came on ahead. *(Looks for a moment at Peg. Hesitantly)* I want to talk to you for a minute … alone! *(All characters on stage move to remotest points and begin to converse. Kevin advances upstage and Peg goes to him)* I don't know how to begin … but I want you to come with me.
Peg	*(Slowly)* I see!
Kevin	I've seen the best and the worst of life in England and I know what loneliness is in a big city. I want to marry you and make a home for you, if you'll have me.
Peg	Why me?
Kevin	I think I know you! You remember the evening we went walking … It was only an hour with you but I know that you're honest and that you'd make a good wife. I have a good position over there and with you I could go a long way. That is why I came early this morning, before the others, to ask you.

Peg	And the baby … *(Kevin turns away)* … But surely you don't expect me to leave my baby. I couldn't do that.
Kevin	After a while … if things work out!
Peg	I see! … Surely you don't expect me to leave my baby. I could not do that!
Kevin	Well, if you can't, we'll take the baby then. Will you?
Peg	No … I don't think so! You don't need me so badly. You'll work out fine.
Kevin	But why? … It's a grand chance for you … you'll never do any good for yourself here.
Peg	I like you, Kevin. You're sensible and ambitious and you know where you're going. *(Shakes head)* But you see, I'm not too keen on sensible men who know where they are going and anyway I made a vow that I'd never send a son of mine to England.
Kevin	*(Indicates Maurice Browne)* Who is it? Your man over there? … He's an alcoholic!
Peg	No! I don't think he is, somehow. He could be. But he isn't one yet.
Kevin	Is it because of him you won't come with me?
Peg	*(Looks askance at Maurice who is watching them)* No! You need not worry. He doesn't think of me like that. *(Maurice advances and joins them)*
Maurice	You can tell me clear out if you like, but I have something to say, too. I take it he asked you to go to England with him?
Kevin	I don't see why you should interrupt a private conversation!
Maurice	I'll tell you why! Because I have a claim to stake, too. *(Turns to Peg and takes her hands)* I want you to come to England with me. I love you and I can't bear the thought of anybody else marrying you, and you're the only hope I have … so now!
Peg	*(Affected but hurt)* Oh, Maurice!
Kevin	And the baby! What about the baby?
Maurice	If she'll have me, I'll have her baby, her father and mother, or anything else she wants.
Peg	You're a fool to go to England, Maurice! You could do so much here. I heard you talking to the TD this morning. You only said what everyone is thinking. You have the guts Maurice, and the education.
Maurice	But I don't want to go! I'll stay here if that's what you want.

	I'll do anything you want me to do. I'll teach in Dublin, Cork, Limerick or Waterford, if you'll marry me. What do you say?
Peg	I say – stick it out here in Keelty, come Hell or high water, TD or no TD.
Maurice	With you behind me, he'd have a job shiftin' me out of Keelty … You'll marry me, Peg?
Peg	Will I, Maurice?
Maurice	Oh, God, I hope you will, Peg.

(Enter Dawheen Timmineen Din, followed by a procession of five, all carrying suitcases. They are his wife, Maynan and Dinny and Dot and another son and daughter Micky and Mary. Micky is approximately sixteen, Mary about fifteen. Micky and Mary are nervous and poorly dressed. DTD orders his retinue to be seated)

DTD	*(To Peg)* A half whiskey, a half o' port wine and two minerals. *(Nudges Dot)* What's for you?
Dot	Gin and It!
DTD	Wouldn't the 'It' be enough for you? *(To Dinny)* What's for you?
Dinny	I'll have a brandy.
DTD	Brandy! Isn't that the last of all! A gin and it and a brandy. *(To Peg, who is absorbed in Maurice)* A gin and it and a brandy. *(Exit Peg. DTD calls Micky and Mary aside)* There's a frightful test before ye over there. Go to bed early at night and talk to no one with a strange accent. Don't forget to send home a few pounds now and again and, above all, don't attempt to ate mate on a Friday.
Maynan	Keep yeerselves to yeerselves and yeer own brothers and sisters over. Call every stranger you meet 'sir!' and look as foolish as you can and don't forget the Hail Marys for a happy death and purity, and praise be all on high ye'll be a credit to yeer father an' mother.
DTD	Don't go spendin' money foolish. Spare every half penny because there'll be a great scarcity o' money before the end o' the year. I saw it in *Old Moore's Almanac*.
Danger	'Twill ruin small farmers!
DTD	No one talkin' to you!
Danger	So you're sendin' another shipment this mornin'. 'Tis worse than the horse trade.

(Enter Peg with drinks which she distributes)

DTD	*(To Dinny)* Pay for that – you called for it. *(Dinny does so. To Maynan)* Drink that up. There's milk for the creamery.
Danger	*(To DTD)* Promise me you won't cry. I couldn't stand it!
DTD	Bum! *(DTD finishes his drink)*
Danger	*(To no one in particular – vehemently)* We'll always be goin' from this miserable country. No one wants us. There's your Ireland for you, with grief and goodbyes and ullagoning at every railway station. *(Passionately)* What honest-to-God politician with an ounce of guts in him would keep his mouth shut when he sees the father of a family goin' away alone with his heart broke, leavin' his poor children behind him. 'Tis the end of the world for them because their father is leavin' them behind. What man, with a drop o' honest blood in his veins, wouldn't rise up an' shout: 'Stop! Stop it! Stop this cruelty. Stop tearin' the hearts out of innocent people! Stop sittin' down on yeer backsides an' do somethin'!'
DTD	*(To Maynan)* Come on! The milk will be sour in the tanks. *(To Mary and Micky)* Say goodbye to yeer mother now! *(Tremulously Mary says goodbye as does Micky. So do Dot, Dinny and Kevin)* Have you the 'Lourdes water'? *(Maynan produces the 'Lourdes water' which she sprinkles over them. She then exits hurriedly)* Don't forget the few pounds, an' God bless ye all!
Kitty:	*(Loudly)* Boo!
	(She is joined by some of the people on stage. Enter Seelie)
Seelie	What's all this racket? What's this bar turning into? *(To Danger)* What are you doing here?
Danger	*(Affected tone)* I'm goin' to England, but I knew you'd be disappointed if I went without sayin' goodbye to you.
Seelie	Good riddance! *(She notices Kitty and the melodeon player)* And you! What are you two doing here? *(To Peg)* Where's Tom?
Peg	I didn't see him this morning.
Seelie	You mean he hasn't shown up at all this morning?
Peg	That's right!
Seelie	And why didn't you call me?
Peg	Well, you were gone to Mass, an' I was too busy.
	(Enter Tom, wearing mackintosh, looking spick and span and carrying a suitcase. With an air of independence he places bag at Seelie's feet)
Tom	*(Loudly)* Peg! A ball o' malt! I have a train to catch.

	(Exit Peg)
Seelie	(*Angrily*) What do you mean – you have a train to catch? Where do you think you're going?
Tom	England!
Seelie	Now, listen to me, Tom Hannigan! You get that silly notion out of your head right away.
Tom	I see nothing silly about it. It might sound silly to yourself and that bunch of Holy Josies you hang around with, but it's a very serious thing to me.
Seelie	(*Alarmed*) What's the matter with you, Tom? Are you feeling all right?
Tom	Never felt better in my life, except that I just copped on to my-self. (*Peg enters and hands him glass of whiskey. He immediately swallows it*) I'm getting old, Seelie. Do you understand that? In another ten years I'll be an old man and what have I done with my life? Damn all! And if I stay here I'll never do anything. I've been a mouse for thirty years. But this morning I copped on to myself. I'm going to England, Seelie, and nothing is going to stop me.
Seelie	But, why? What put this madness into your head so sud-denly? You might have let me know!
Tom	I didn't know myself until this morning. I could never get married here.
Seelie	You don't know what you're doing! It's the drink!
Tom	Oh, I know what I'm doing all right! I know at last.
Seelie	But you have everything you want here.
Tom	No, Seelie, I haven't! You have! You have your Mass every morning and your devotions every evening. But I'm different, Seelie. I'm weak. I want flesh and blood. Maybe I'll meet a girl that'll take to me. Maybe I'll turn out like other fellows and be married and have a wife to look after me. 'Tis only fair, Seelie. You'll probably tell me to go to Hell, but I can tell you – go to Heaven!
Danger	'Twon't be much fun up there if they're all like her.
Seelie	Oh! … wait till I tell Fr Madigan. (*Exit Seelie*)
Tom	I knew she'd say exactly that!
Dot	Anybody got the time? My watch has stopped!
Johnny	We have thirteen minutes to be exact.
Danger	We'd better be gettin' ready. I never thought I'd see the day

I'd be leavin' Ireland. *(Assumes a stentorian tone, military-like)* All right, my lads! Form a line here! *(They form a line across the stage. The line consists of those who are going to England. Peg and Maurice Browne stand at one side. Kitty and melodeon player stand behind line. Loudly)* Number off! *(They number off)* Tenshun! *(They stand to attention. Falsetto)* We are not the first and we will not be the last. God help us! Chins up an' let me see smiles on those faces. Don't blame poor oul' Ireland but blame the hypocrites that brought us to this pass. Come on, Kitty. Play us up to the station. Your song, Peg, before we go. *(Peg comes forward)*

Peg   *(Singing)* Many young men of twenty said goodbye
All that long day
From break of dawn until the sun was high
Many young men of twenty said goodbye
They left the mountain and the glen
The lassies and the fine young men
I saw the tears of every girl and boy
Many young men of twenty said goodbye.

Danger   All together!

All   *(Singing)* Many young men of twenty said goodbye
All that long day
From break of dawn until the sun was high
They left the mountain and the glen
The lassies and the fine young men
I saw the tears of every girl and boy
Many young men of twenty said goodbye
Many young men of twenty said goodbye.

Kitty   We'll play you up to the station. Start up the music Davy.
(Singing the last verse over again, they exit led by Kitty and Davy, the melodeon player, who plays the tune on his melodeon. The last line of the song is repeated until it fades out and on the stage Maurice Browne and Peg Finnerty embrace)

(FINAL CURTAIN)

MANY YOUNG MEN OF TWENTY

BLACK PUDDIN' SONG

MIKEY HOULIHAN

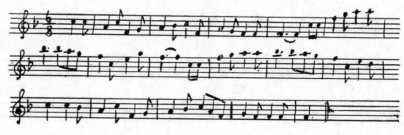

SERVANT GIRL

DAWN IN KEELTY

KITTY CURLEY